SMITHSONIAN INSTITUTION
BUREAU OF AMERICAN ETHNOLOGY
BULLETIN 79

BLOOD REVENGE, WAR, AND VICTORY FEASTS AMONG THE JIBARO INDIANS OF EASTERN ECUADOR

BY

RAFAEL KARSTEN

WASHINGTON
GOVERNMENT PRINTING OFFICE
1923

30212

LETTER OF TRANSMITTAL

SMITHSONIAN INSTITUTION,
BUREAU OF AMERICAN ETHNOLOGY,
Washington, D. C., February 1, 1921.

SIR: I have the honor to transmit herewith the manuscript of a paper entitled "Blood revenge, war, and victory feasts among the Jibaro Indians of Eastern Ecuador," by Rafael Karsten, and to recommend its publication, subject to your approval, as a bulletin of this bureau.

Very respectfully,

J. WALTER FEWKES, *Chief.*

Dr. CHARLES D. WALCOTT,
Secretary of the Smithsonian Institution.

CONTENTS

CONTENTS

ILLUSTRATIONS

BLOOD REVENGE, WAR, AND VICTORY FEASTS AMONG THE JIBARO INDIANS OF EASTERN ECUADOR

By Rafael Karsten

INTRODUCTION

The Jibaro Indians, who in their own language are called *Shuára*, inhabit the virgin forests around the great rivers Pastaza, Morona, Upano-Santiago and their affluents, regions politically divided between the Republics of Ecuador and Peru, and still form one of the most numerous and most important Indian tribes of South America. Although some Jibaros live in parts of the country to which no white man has yet penetrated, their present total number can without exaggeration be estimated at fifteen or twenty thousand. The Jibaros are divided into a number of smaller tribes which are generally hostile to each other. They have no uniform tribal organization and do not recognize any common political authority. This division also stamps their social institutions and customs, which are somewhat different among different tribes. Against the whites the Jibaros have, in critical times, been able to maintain themselves as a united and homogeneous nation. The best proof of this is the general insurrection which, on account of the oppression of the Spaniards, was carried out in 1599 by all tribes living on the Upano, Paute, Santiago, and Morona, and at which the majority of the white population in the flourishing villages Sevilla de Oro, Logroño, and Mendoza were massacred by the Indians. Since that time the whites have, on the whole, left the Jibaros unmolested, but between themselves they have continued those destructive wars which more than anything else have contributed to the diminution of the Jibaro race.

The Jibaros no doubt at present are the most warlike of all Indian tribes in South America. The wars, the blood-feuds within the tribes, and the wars of extermination between the different tribes are continuous, being nourished by their superstitious belief in witchcraft. These wars are the greatest curse of the Jibaros and are felt to be so even by themselves, at least so far as the feuds within the tribes are concerned. On the other hand, the wars are to

1

such a degree one with their whole life and essence that only powerful pressure from outside or a radical change of their whole character and moral views could make them abstain from them. This one may judge even from the fact that from a victory over his enemies the Jibaro warrior not only expects honor and fame in the ordinary sense of the word but also certain material benefits. The head trophy which he takes from his slain enemy is not merely a token of victory, but becomes a fetish charged with supernatural power, and the great victory feast itself with its many mysterious ceremonies, in fact, forms a part of the practical religion or cult of the Jibaros.

The education of the boys among the Jibaros first of all aims at making them brave and skillful warriors. When a Jibaro has enemies on whom he wants to take revenge for offences and outrages, perhaps committed long ago, but despairs of being able to do it himself, he systematically tries to awaken and maintain hatred against them in his young sons by discourses directed to them every day. " The *Shuāra* So-and-so killed my father, my grandfather, my brothers, while I was a child, carried off my mother, my sisters, and burnt our house. This blood guilt is not yet washed off. It is the duty of you, my sons, to avenge this crime and to kill the enemy or his sons, who are still threatening our family. If you do this, blessing and good luck will follow you in all your undertakings; you will have a long life and be able to kill many other enemies; your plantations will be richly fruit-bearing; your domestic animals, the swine and the chicken, will prosper and grow numerous; there will never be lack of food in your house," etc. This discourse is, at times, repeated every morning when the house father gets up, and with about the same words; and, of course, can not fail to make an impression upon the minds of the young ones.

When a Jibaro chief goes on a war expedition he often takes his young sons with him in order that they may early learn the art of war and get accustomed to the bloody scenes which take place.

When a boy reaches the age of puberty and is to be received among the full-grown men, a feast is made in his honor which is called *kusúpani* and which chiefly consists in ceremonies with tobacco. After the feast, which lasts three or four days, he is obliged to take a narcotic drink, called *maikoa*, prepared from the rind of the bush *Datura arborea*. This bush seems to have much the same poisonous properties as belladonna or opium, and the drink prepared from its rind has the power of completely narcotizing the Indian as well as awakening within him peculiar visions and hallucinations which are ascribed to certain spirits. The most important of these spirits are the so-called *arutama* ("the old ones") which are in their nature the souls of the ancestors. These appear in all sorts of terrible shapes, as tigers, eagles, giant snakes, and other wild animals, or reveal their presence in stupendous phenomena of nature, in the lightning, in the rainbow, in meteors, etc. They speak to the young Jibaro and advise and teach him in all kinds of manly businesses, but first of all in warlike deeds. Only the Jibaro youth who has seen the *arútama* in the dream and has been spoken to by them can expect to become a valiant and successful warrior, to kill many enemies, and himself secure long life. When afterwards in real life he meets a tiger, an eagle, a boa serpent, or some other wild animal he shows no fright and does not flee, but bravely challenges it with his lance. Similarly in the fight he without fear meets his enemy.

Even older warriors who want to know who their enemies are and whether in a war against them they will be victorious are in the habit of drinking either *maikoa* or another narcotic drink, prepared from the stem of the vine *Banisteria caapi* and called *natéma*. *Maikoa*, the effects of which are much stronger, is, however, the particular narcotic of warriors. If one asks a Jibaro why he drinks *maikoa* he generally answers: "I do it in order to kill my enemies" (*Shuára mátinyu*). The Jibaro warrior generally receives the revelations of the spirits while sleeping alone in the virgin forest in a small ranch made of palm leaves, usually situated many miles away from the habitations of the Indians.

MEANS OF DEFENSE

That the Jibaros are professional warriors also appears from the way in which they construct their houses and from the defensive measures to which they have recourse when particularly threatened by their enemies. The Jibaros, like other Indian tribes inhabiting the virgin forests of Amazonas, do not live in villages but in sundry large communal houses in which several families of near relations may find room. Such a house (called *héa*) is generally situated on a high hill from which it is easy to dominate the surrounding country, or in the angle of a river, which protects it from two or three sides. Besides, the Jibaros rarely settle at the banks of the main rivers, but prefer to make their houses at small affluents of these in the interior of the country. Thus they not only avoid the whites, who now and then travel along the great rivers, but are also better protected against hostile Indian tribes.

The houses themselves are constructed with great care, and even in times of peace are provided with walls of strong chonta poles (pl. 1). When a family is particularly threatened by enemies, the house is fortified in a special way. On the outer side of the ordinary wall another wall is made, consisting of big chonta stems, so that the house has two walls, one close to the other. Within the houses, all along the walls, a number of small rooms or partitions, about 1 meter in height, are likewise made of chonta poles, each having a small hole in the outside through which the warrior can shoot his attacking enemy. There is one such small room for each defender of the house. The partitions will afford the warrior protection in case the enemy are able to penetrate into the house. As to the doors, there are two in each Jibaro house, one at each end of the house, one for the men, the other for the women. These doors generally consist of six chonta poles, the upper ends of which are united by means of strong lianas, while the nether ends are free and can be separated from each other, three to each side, making an opening of triangular form. The whole opening is so small, however, that only one man at a time with some difficulty can enter the house. During the night the poles forming the doors are always carefully closed and fastened by a transverse pole applied to the inner side, so that the entrance of undesirable persons is made impossible. Even the outer wall in a fortified house has a special door consisting of similar poles which can be closed from the inside.

Not only the houses themselves but also the manioc and banana plantations situated close by are protected in a similar way by high fences of strong chonta poles. The aim of this arrangement is to prevent the enemy from approaching the house through the plantations.

Formerly, before the use of firearms was so general among the Jibaros as it is now, the chiefs especially were in the habit of constructing a sort of war tower at one end of their houses. These towers were of quadratic form and sometimes 30 or 40 meters in height. On the top of it there was a small room about 4 meters in quadrate and with walls about 1 meter in height, made of strong chonta poles, which protected the defender against the lances of the enemies. The whole thing rested upon pillars of the stem of the chonta palm, and the warrior ascended along a stair consisting of wooden logs with incisions which gave him foothold. These war towers were called *kumbínta*. After the Jibaros began to make use of firearms in their wars these measures of defense proved less fit for the purpose, and consequently were no longer used.

It is still common among the Jibaros to arrange a kind of trap on the way which leads to the house and where one expects the enemy will try to approach it. One such trap consists of a round hole in the ground, about 1½ meters deep and large enough for a full-grown man to fall into it. At the bottom of the hole three pointed sticks of chonta, resembling points of lances, are arranged in an erect position. These pointed sticks are called *āshi*. The part which

a. An unfortified Jibaro house

b. The interior of a Jibaro house

A TRAP IN THE VIRGIN FOREST

b. Jibaro women

a. Jibaro men

b. Jibaro warrior

a. Jibaro youths

sticks out from the earth has a length of about half a meter. At the surface of the earth the opening of the hole is covered with small sticks and leaves which makes it difficult or impossible for the enemy, creeping along in the darkness, to discover its presence before he falls into it. When he falls his feet are transfixed by the pointed sticks and he is not able to get out. Besides, the defenders of the house are often keeping watch at these holes, ready to dispatch the enemy when he is caught in them. The Jibaros call these traps *mesértinyu whuā*, " a hole of death."

Another kind of trap, which likewise is arranged on the narrow path leading to the house, is the following : It consists of a small tree, growing close to the path, which is bent down, or of a big branch of a tree, one end of which is fixed in the ground so that with the latter it forms an angle of about 30°. To the upper end of this branch eight pointed chonta sticks are attached in such a way that they form as it were a comb. The branch is bent back like a bow against a couple of poles fixed in the ground for the purpose, to which it is attached by means of a strong liana in a certain ingenious way that can not be fully described in words. Across the path a few inches over the ground another liana is stretched and tied at one of the poles just mentioned. Between this liana and the liana holding the bent branch there is such a connection that when the foot of the enemy touches the former, the bow is released, and the comb with the pointed chonta sticks will strike him with terrible force in the face or the chest. The liana stretched across the path is sometimes covered with leaves in order that the enemy may not notice it, but besides, even this weapon is calculated to operate mainly in the darkness, since the attacks are nearly always made at night. The trap described (pl. 2) is called *tambūnchi* by the Jibaros and *singbrāru* by the Quichua-speaking Canelos Indians.

Whereas the *tambūnchi* has been used by the Jibaros since ancient times, the following defensive measure is of modern origin : Across the path along which the enemy is expected to come a blackened string is stretched at such a height that it reaches a man to the chest. At the tree where one end of the string is fastened a charged and cocked rifle is tied, with the barrel fixed in the direction of the string. The end of the string is brought in such a connection with the trigger of the rifle that when the enemy, coming along in the darkness, gives it a push, the shot is discharged and is likely to hit him in the chest. Even if he should escape from being hit, the shot would warn the inhabitants of the house that enemies were approaching.

The big signal drum of the Jibaros, called *tundúi*, also plays a part in the wars, although originally it seems to have been a purely religious instrument. At times when there is fear of an attack of enemies it is placed outside the house on the hill, and the beats may then be heard at a distance of several miles. The drum *tundúi* is beaten partly when the Jibaros drink the narcotics *maikoa* and *natéma*—in which case the object is to summon the spirits that inhabit these sacred drinks—partly after a death, and lastly to give the friends notice of an attack of enemies. In the latter case the signaling consists of a series of short and fast beats at a time which is at first forte or fortissimo and thereafter gradually diminishes. When the friends in the other houses hear these beats they say: *Pakinmawui*, "they are killing." Hence this whole mode of signaling is called *pakinmawui*. As soon as the inhabitants in a house get knowledge of or suspect the presence of enemies, and also during the attack, if there is time for it, they try by beating the *tundúi* to summon their friends for rescue, and the signaling may sometimes cause the enemy, fearing the arrival of help, to give up his evil intention and take flight.

The principal weapons of war of the Jibaro Indians are the lance (*nánki*) and the shield (*tandára*), the former being used for attack, the latter for defense. Nowadays the Jibaros, besides these weapons, also commonly use firearms (*akáru*) received from the whites, generally in exchange for a human head (*tsántsa*). The lance should be made of the hard wood of the chonta palm, if possible the kind of chonta cultivated by the Jibaros (called *uí*). The head is of prismatic shape and with the shaft forms a single piece. Anciently the Jibaros also used lance heads made of the leg bones of the tiger or the bear, which were fitted into shafts of chonta. A special power is ascribed to the chonta lance, owing to the belief that the spiny chonta palm itself is a demoniac tree, the seat of a spirit (*wakáni* or *iguánchi*). The chonta lance therefore inspires not only men but also the spirits and demons with fear. Hence at the *tsántsa* feast the head trophy is always kept tied to a chonta lance at those moments when it is not needed for the ceremonies.

The shield is made of a special kind of wood which the Jibaros call *kamáka*, the Quichua-speaking Canelos Indians *lancháma*, and which has the property of being at once light and strong. It is always round and wrought of one single piece, although the shields are sometimes very large. During the days the Jibaro makes the rough work he partly fasts, especially abstaining from eating a kind of sweet potatoes (*Convolvulus batatas*), called *inchi* by the Jibaros. If he eats this fruit the shield will be attacked by moth, rot, and become useless. This superstition is due to the fact that the sweet potato has the same appearance as moth-eaten or rotten wood. During the same days the Jibaro likewise abstains from cohabiting with his wives, for if he has intercourse with a woman the shield will burst or get crooked.

The Canelos Indians, who in part are of the same race as the Jibaros, at the making of the shield observe the following rules: The rough work is carried out in four days. The Indian works every day from early morning until noon. During the whole forenoon, until the work is finished for that day, the Indian fasts and does not eat or drink anything. As soon as the work is finished at noon he drinks chicha (manioc beer), and in the afternoon he may also eat other kinds of food. While working upon the shield he observes the rule not to speak to anybody, but keeps strict silence. Nor does he, during the four days and nights, cohabit with his wife. If he infringes these rules the shield will get humpy or burst, or be attacked by moth.

As soon as the shield is made it is often painted on the outside with the black dye obtained from the genipa fruit, called *sua* by the Jibaros. The patterns represent spirits (*wakáni supai*), giant snakes (*pangi, amárun*), butterflies (*wambishku*), and other animals. These patterns are supposed to inspire the enemy with fear and to give strength and courage to the warrior himself.

The Jibaros use shields of two kinds. Some are very large and somewhat heavy and are used only for defense within the house. The shield rests against the ground or against a round seat of the kind the Jibaros use, and the warrior with his lance tries to defend himself against the enemy penetrating into the house. Other kinds of shields are smaller and lighter and are carried by the Indians on war expeditions.

The Jibaros never use blowpipes and poisoned arrows in their wars, but only for hunting. They believe that if they kill a man with a poisoned arrow that poison will no longer do for killing an animal or bird of the forest. Besides, it seems that the poisoned arrows are not regarded as a sufficiently effective weapon to fight men with. The Indian, when killing his enemy, desires to inflict as large wounds and to shed as much blood as possible, a fact that explains his predilection for the lance as a weapon of war.

CHIEFS AND WARS

Among the Jibaros (pls. 3, 4) each family father is theoretically absolute ruler over his house people, and in times of peace there is no recognized common chief even within the tribe, and still less any exercising authority over several tribes. The Jibaros have not even a proper name for a chief. The word *capitu*, which is sometimes used, is borrowed from the Spanish and is used principally to denote a white man of importance. It is only in times of war that a chieftainship exists; that is to say, during those great wars of extermination which are carried out against other Jibaro tribes. Such a temporary chief of war is generally only called *unta*, "the old one," because the chiefs are nearly always old, experienced men who have killed many enemies and captured many heads. The small blood feuds within the tribe, on the other hand, have a more private character and as a rule are not fought out under the leadership of a common chief.

The dignity of a chieftain is hereditary in a relative sense, in so far that the son of a chief is generally elected a chief in time of war after his father has died or grown decrepit. This, however, can only take place in case he has proved a valiant and skilled warrior and has killed enemies. No Jibaro is selected as a chief if he has not killed at least one enemy. The Jibaros have absolute faith in the heritability of prominent qualities, and ascribe an extraordinary importance to education and the power of example. The son of a great chief, they say, must necessarily also become an able warrior because he is, as it were, a direct continuation of his father, has received a careful education for the deeds of war, and has always had the good example of his great father before his eyes.

The authority of the chief elected for a war is very great. It is he alone who disposes everything for the expedition planned, who decides about the time for and the mode of making the attack, and the younger warriors oblige themselves to obey him in everything. But as soon as a war has been carried to a successful end the power of the chief ceases, and he has, in spite of the great repute he always enjoys, no more authority or right to decide over the doings of his tribesmen than any other family father among the Jibaros.

CAUSES OF THE WARS

Before describing the modes of making war among the Jibaro Indians it is necessary to state what the causes of these wars generally are.

The Jibaros are by nature impulsive and choleric, qualities that among them frequently give rise to disputes and quarrels which may degenerate into sanguinary feuds. Their unbounded sense of liberty and their desire to be independent, not only of the whites but also of each other, is one of the reasons why they do not live in villages but each family separately, for in this way conflicts are more easily avoided. It may, for instance, happen that the swine, the most important domestic animals, who during the day are allowed to roam about freely in the forest, penetrate into the plantations of a neighboring family and devastate the crops. The owner gets angry and claims compensation for the damage done. In this way quarrels easily arise which may develop into bloody fights; at any rate there enters general discord and distrust between the two families. Some

time later it may happen that one or more members of either family fall ill with some of the diseases which the Jibaros ascribe to witchcraft. When trying to find out the author of the evil the head of that family is most likely to attribute it to the malicious art of a neighbor with whom he has had such a quarrel. If the patient dies he has recourse to divination by means of the narcotic *natéma,* which generally leads to his suspicions against the neighbor being confirmed. The family's sense of justice as well as the duty to the deceased now require that revenge shall be taken, and the supposed wizard is assassinated. This murder naturally awakes the desire for blood revenge on the part of the family thus outraged, and so a blood feud is begun which, as is easily understood, has a tendency to make itself permanent.

Since supposed sorcery is nearly always the nearest cause of murders within the tribe, it is clear that the professional sorcerers or medicine men are those members of Jibaro society which are most frequently exposed to the revengeful attacks of their enemies. As a matter of fact, in large Indian societies sorcerers are almost continually assassinated, or at least threatened with death, by their enemies. When a medicine man has undertaken to cure a sick person and the latter dies in spite of the treatment, the "doctor" is also generally made responsible for the death, the relatives of the dead reasoning that the medicine man, instead of curing the patient, on the contrary used his art to kill him. The unsuccessful curer is therefore murdered unless he escapes by flight. Since the Jibaros, on the whole, do not recognize what we call a natural death but always attribute a death to supernatural causes, any death among them tends to give rise to a murder, the relatives of the deceased considering it as their duty to take revenge upon the supposed author of the accident.

It must, however, be remarked that among the Jibaros the professional medicine men are not the only persons who know about sorcery and witchcraft. Most old men, and especially the chiefs, are more or less initiated in the art.

The Jibaros make a distinction between evil caused by witchcraft (*túnchi*) and disease (*súngura*). The illness of a patient is generally attributed to witchcraft when it consists in violent pains in some part of the body, especially when the pain is accompanied by swelling of that part. Thus, for instance, headache, rheumatic pains, and colic are ascribed to witchcraft. On the other hand, to the category " disease " (*súngura*) the Jibaros set down especially such illnesses as have originally been brought to them by the whites and which are not particularly accompanied by pains, like dysentery, smallpox, and most other fever diseases. Now, if somebody has "brought sickness," *i. e.,* contagion, to the house of another Jibaro so that some member of the family falls ill and dies, that person is also exposed to the revenge of the relatives. They are perhaps ready to admit that he has not caused the evil intentionally, but this circumstance does not free him from responsibility and from the obligation of at least paying a material compensation for the positive loss he has caused to the family which through him has been deprived of a useful member. In a case like this, therefore, compensation may enter instead of blood revenge. In the same way the Indian is apt to recognize extenuating circumstances even in other cases where the evil has not been caused willfully—for instance, when somebody in a state of drunkenness or under the influence of a narcotic drink has been the cause of another person's death. If, on the other hand, the doer refuses to pay compensation, blood revenge is likely to be carried out against him.

Again, in cases where the evil intention is prominent, the moral indignation aroused by the deed is so much greater, and particularly witchery is regarded as so grave and unpardonable a crime, that it can be atoned by blood only.

Not seldom bloody feuds arise among the Jibaros for the sake of the women. The Jibaros live in polygamy and hold their wives in high estimation. The women, as a matter of fact, have much to say in Jibaro society and are generally treated well. The men, however, are very jealous of their wives and adultery is severely punished, the husband maltreating his unfaithful wife with the lance or a knife so as to sometimes cause her death. In such cases, however, the relatives of the woman frequently take her part, alleging that she is innocent. If in their opinion she has been punished wrongfully or with undue severity, they try to take a corresponding revenge upon her husband. Under such circumstances more than one Jibaro has been killed by his father-in-law or his brothers-in-law. Thus on the Rio Upáno a young Jibaro had once taken the life of his wife on account of unfaithfulness, real or supposed, on her part. Some time afterwards the cruelly mutilated dead body of the Indian was found in the forest. He had been murdered by the relatives of his former wife. Ordinary captures of women, which frequently take place among the Jibaros, also give rise to blood feuds. A Jibaro carries off the wife of another Indian or takes her with her own consent. The offended husband summons his friends and starts to persecute the seducer to kill him. If under such circumstances a murder has been committed, this usually causes a new murder from the party offended, and so on, until either all grown-up members of one family have been exterminated, or, what happens more generally, each party gets tired of the feud and they decide to leave one another in peace. Sometimes the affair is settled by a formal agreement.

The Jibaro Indian is wholly penetrated by the idea of retaliation; his desire for revenge is an expression of his sense of justice. This principle is eye for eye, tooth for tooth, life for life. If one reprefiends a Jibaro because he has killed an enemy, his answer is generally: "He has killed himself." But blood revenge among these Indians is not merely owing to moral or ethical, but also to religious reasons. The soul of the murdered Indian requires that his relatives shall avenge his death. The errant spirit, which gets no rest, visits his sons, his brothers, his father, in the dream, and, weeping, conjures them not to let the slayer escape but to wreak vengeance upon him for the life he has taken. If they omit to fulfill this duty the anger of the vengeful spirit may turn against themselves. To avenge the blood of a murdered father, brother, or son, is therefore looked upon as one of the most sacred duties of a Jibaro Indian. The expression which the Jibaros use for this is *ayambruamáktinyu* (in Quichua *randipashca*) which means "to avenge the blood of a murdered relation." It may happen that a Jibaro keeps the thought of revenge in his mind for years, even for decades, waiting for the opportunity to carry it out, but he never gives it up. A man has perhaps been murdered while his sons were still small, and he has perhaps likewise lacked brothers or other male relatives who had been able to revenge his death. As soon as the sons become full grown they know what their duty toward their murdered father requires of them. However, in such cases it sometimes occurs that the affair is settled in a peaceful way. The sons of the murdered Indian send the following message to the slayer, or, in case he is dead, to his sons: "You (or your father) killed our father while we were still children. It is our duty to avenge his blood and to take your life in retaliation. But if you promise to pay such and such a price— a rifle, an axe, a good hound, etc.—we will regard the blood guilt as atoned and pardon you." If the Indian thus threatened agrees with this, the matter is definitely settled. The Jibaros do not find anything repugnant in thus estimating the life of a parent with material equivalents, and an agreement like this is especially possible in cases where the crime to be punished has been committed very long ago. In cases of murder recently committed the indignation of the offended family is generally so great that any material compensation is out of the question, and an atonement in blood is required.

Among the Jibaros blood revenge is not strictly individualized in the sense that it always directs itself exclusively against the slayer. The Jibaro certainly first of all wants to take revenge on the person who committed the crime, but if he can not be caught it may instead be directed against some one of his relatives—his brother, his father, even his mother or sister. To understand this we have to consider that the conception of individual personality and consequently of individual responsibility does not exist among the primitive Indians in the same sense as among civilized peoples. The individual forms an inseparable part of a whole, namely, of the family or tribe to which he belongs. Especially the members of the same family are regarded as, so to speak, organically coherent with each other, so that one part stands for all and all for one. What happens to one member of that social unit happens to all, and for the deed of one member the rest are held equally responsible. How the Jibaros conceive this connection appears from certain of their social customs. For instance, custom requires that after a child is born the parents shall fast and observe other rules of abstinence for a couple of years, or until the child is named. This is due to the idea that something of the souls or essence of the parents inheres in the child, so that all three in one way form a single organism, a single personality. But this mystic connection between the parents and the child also subsists after the child has grown up, although perhaps less intimately. Similarly the tie which unites brothers and sisters in a family is so intimate that they may be said together to form one organic whole. Among the Jibaros and the Canelos Indians, when one member of the family is sick the rest have to diet in the same way as the patient himself, for if they eat unsuitable food it would be the same as if the patient ate that food, and his condition would grow worse. From the same point of view we have to explain the custom prevailing among the Jibaros that when a man dies his brother must marry the widow. The departed husband, who is still jealous of the wife he left behind, does not cede her to any other man than his brother, who with himself forms one personality and represents him in the most real sense of the word. When a younger Jibaro is murdered by his enemies the duty of revenging his death is also first of all incumbent on his brothers.

The Jibaro can not even distinguish his own personality from his material belongings; at least not from things he has made himself. When he fabricates a shield, a drum, a blowpipe, or some other delicate object, he has to diet and observe abstinence in other ways; for, according to his own idea, he actually puts something of his own personality, his own soul, into the object he is making. His own properties, both the essential and habitual ones and those occasionally acquired through eating a certain food, etc., will therefore be transferred to that object. The division of labor existing among the Indians depends on the same peculiar view. Thus, for instance, the Indian woman has to fabricate the clay vessels and manages these utensils, because the clay of which they are made, like the earth itself, is female—that is, has a woman's soul. She is connected with the fire and has to cook the food, because the fire has a female soul, etc.

Such a view prevailing among the Indians, it is easy to understand that a Jibaro, with regard to the murder of one of his relatives, asks not so much which individual has committed the deed, but rather reasons in the following way: "A member of that family has murdered my relative; consequently, in revenge, some member of that family must die."

When a murder committed by an own tribesman is to be avenged, the social morals of the Jibaros require that the punishment shall be meted out with justice, in so far that for one life which has been taken only one life should be taken in retaliation. Thereupon, the blood guilt is atoned (*tumáshi akérkama*) and the offended family is satisfied. Consequently, if a Jibaro Indian wishes to revenge a murder of his brother, it may well happen that he, in case the slayer himself can not be caught and punished, will assassinate his brother or father instead of him, but he does not take the life of more than one member of the family, even if he has an opportunity of killing more. If he, for instance, killed not only the murderer himself but also some one of his brothers, this would awaken indignation in the whole tribe, and it would be considered righteous that the family thus offended in its turn should take revenge. The blood guilt in such a case has passed to the original avenger. This principle, which requires that there shall be justice in the retaliation so that life is weighed against life, of course, in itself has a tendency to limit blood revenge. It happens, however, in many cases, and especially with regard to supposed witchery, that the person accused of the crime does not admit the guilt but asserts that he and his family are innocently persecuted by the relatives of the dead. If, then, he or a member of his family is murdered, his relatives try, in their turn, to take revenge, and so on, in which case the blood feud tends to become prolonged indefinitely.

If thus, as we have seen, among the Jibaros blood revenge takes place even with regard to members of the same tribe, it fails when such a crime is committed within the family. Among these Indians it sometimes occurs that a man kills his brother, if the latter, for instance, has seduced his wife or bewitched one of his children. But in this case blood revenge generally fails, inasmuch as the natural avengers—that is, the father and the remaining brothers—abstain from carrying it out. "It is enough that one member of our family has died," they say, "why should we deprive ourselves of one more?" The slayer is consequently pardoned. The failing of blood revenge in a case like this is due to the natural sympathy which the avengers feel for the slayer, as well as to the consideration that by killing him they would only harm themselves by weakening the power and influence of the family.

That the blood feuds which take place within the tribe have an entirely different character from the wars of extermination waged against foreign tribes also appears from the fact that only in the latter case, but not in the former, the victors make trophies (*tsantsas*) of the heads of their slain enemies. Such trophies are prepared only of the heads of enemies belonging to a wholly different tribe, with whom the victors do not reckon blood relationship. Consequently, when a Jibaro kills a sorcerer or some other enemy of the same tribe as himself, he leaves the dead body lying where it falls, but he does not cut off his head to make a *tsantsa* of it, saying: "He was of my own people, my own tribe" (*winya eintsu*). Nor is there any victory feast in this case. This principle is so strictly observed that if among a hostile tribe, against which war is waged, there happens to be a person who originally has belonged to the tribe of the assailants—he having for instance been captured from the latter during an earlier war—or one who is descended from such a person, the assailants, if victorious, abstain from taking that person's head, reckoning that he is related to some man of their own tribe. "He was of our own people," they say. The victors may kill him if they are able to do it, but they make no trophy of his head. A Jibaro warrior who did this would run the risk of being killed by his own tribesmen, and, more strictly speaking, by those who reckoned blood relationship with the victim. In such cases, as a matter of fact, disputes sometimes arise between the victors themselves, some wishing to take the head of the killed enemy, whereas others, asserting they are related to him by the tie of blood, are opposed to it. The making of a *tsantsa* of an enemy's head, and especially the feast which follows the acquiring of such a trophy, implies the grossest insult, not only to the murdered person himself and his family, but to his whole tribe. Besides, the so-called *tsantsa* feast, which requires great preparations for years, can only take place where the victor stays far from the vengeful tribesmen of his slain enemy and is safe from their machinations.

Between the different tribes in the regions inhabited by the Jibaros there exists almost perpetual enmity and destructive wars are often carried out, especially between neighboring tribes. The tribes on the Rio Paute thus are generally hostile to those living on the Rio Upano and Santiago and the latter, in their turn, to the tribes inhabiting the vast regions around the Morona and the Pastaza. The tribes of the Rio Chiguaza, a small affluent of the upper Pastaza, are mortal enemies of the Jibaros living on the Rio Capotaza between the upper Pastaza and Bobonaza. All wild Jibaros on the Pastaza have during many years waged real wars of extermination against the half-civilized Canelos Indians on the Bobonaza, and so on. It is not easy to state what originally has been the cause of this enmity. Generally speaking, one may say that it has originated in the jealousy and rivalry existing between the different tribes, a rivalry personalized in the proud and ambitious chiefs who stand at the head of the different tribes. One chief tries to surpass another one in war-like deeds and can not endure seeing his rival increase in wealth, power, and influence. Again, the enmity of the wild Indians against the Canelos Indians seems to be due chiefly to the latter having submitted themselves to the Christian influences and in making themselves dependent upon the whites. But, in addition to this, even with regard to the hostility reigning between the different tribes, superstition—the belief in witchcraft—plays its fatal part, this being nearly always the principal cause of the wars. The rival chiefs combat each other not merely by natural means, but also with the supernatural weapon which is called *túnchi* (in Quichua *chunta*), for a great Jibaro chief is as skilled in witchcraft as a professional sorcerer. In order to bewitch a person it is, according to the idea of the Indians, not absolutely necessary that one should be quite near the victim. Those sorcerers and chiefs who are experienced in the art are able to send the fatal arrow a long distance, often many miles. If, in a tribe and especially within the family of the chief, in a short time various cases of disease, death, or accidents of other kinds occur, these are generally set down to the evil machinations of the sorcerers in a hostile neighboring tribe. Thus, for instance, the Jibaro chief Nayapi on the Pastaza, and the old Canelos chief Palati on the Bobonaza have for many years been enemies and have sent menacing messages to each other. In the family of Nayapi within a comparatively short time several deaths took place— two of his sons, one daughter, and his son-in-law dying from mysterious diseases or through accidents. Nayapi said that his enemy Palati was the cause of all these deaths by systematically letting off his witchery arrows against Nayapi and his family. Palati, again, by no means denied that this was so, but, on the contrary, confirmed it, menacingly announcing that he would, by and by, exterminate Nayapi's whole family. The latter was seized with wrath and desire for revenge, and certainly would have wreaked a terrible vengeance upon his enemy if regard for the Catholic monks, under whose protection Palati stood, had not made him abstain from carrying it out. It may be added that the Canelos Indians, although Christians by name, are known as exceedingly clever witches, even the savage Jibaros acknowledging their superiority to themselves in this art.

Often the hostility between two tribes is only latent, becoming suddenly active through some occasional incident, when a war ensues. Thus, as already mentioned, a series of deaths, which are attributed to the evil art of the treacherous enemy, may occasion a war. It also occurs that an Indian, traveling through the territory of a foreign tribe, with which his own stands on no friendly terms, is assassinated by these secret enemies of his own people, who can not abstain from taking the opportunity. Such an occasional assassination may be the signal for a general war of extermination between the two tribes. This was, for instance, the original cause of the war which, during my sojourn on the Rio Upano, was carried out between some tribes of the Upano and the Santiago on one side, and the Huambiza Indians on the Morona on the other. The son of an influential Indian on the Rio Santiago had, on account of some old quarrel, been murdered while traveling through the land of the Huambiza Indians. The tribesmen of the murdered Indian applied to the Jibaros on the Upano for assistance. The assistance was given, some 40 Upano Indians going down the river to join their friends on the Santiago and marching with them against the Huambizas.

Whereas the small feuds within the tribes have the character of a private blood revenge, based on the principle of just retaliation, the wars between the different tribes are in principle wars of extermination. In these there is no question about weighing life against life; the aim is to completely annihilate the inimical tribe, all members of which form one organic whole and are animated by the same feelings and mode of thought. The victorious party is all the more anxious to leave no single person of the enemy's people, not even small children, alive, as it is feared lest these should later appear as avengers against the victors. As already pointed out, it is also solely in such wars against foreign tribes that trophies are made of the heads of the enemies killed.

Although the wars of the Jibaro Indians are in their nature nothing but wars of revenge, they never aim at territorial conquests. The Jibaros, on the contrary, fear and detest the country of their enemies, where secret supernatural dangers may threaten them even after they have conquered their natural enemies. The sorcerers of the hostile tribe may have left their witching arrows everywhere, on the road, in the forest, in the houses, with the result that the invading enemies may be hit by them when they least expect it. The land of the enemy is therefore abandoned as soon as possible. Besides, the Jibaros who inhabit endless virgin forests, where they can make new settlements almost anywhere, have no need of conquering the territory of other tribes.

HOW THE FEUDS AND WARS ARE CARRIED OUT

Having seen how the wars originate among the Jibaros, we will now examine in detail how these wars are carried out.

When among the Jibaros a family father, especially a chief or a great warrior, dies, and a medicine-man, by drinking *natéma*, has established not only that death has been caused by witchcraft but also who the wizard is, it is incumbent on his nearest male relations, and first of all on his sons, to take revenge on the supposed assassin. At the deathbed of the father they make a solemn promise to fulfill this duty. Often the sons alone carry out the sanguinary business. In case the sorcerer has many defenders they conjoin the brothers or other male relatives of the deceased. Sometimes the conspirators also ask the advice of the chief of the tribe, but the latter generally does not take part in such a private feud unless he has some personal interest in it.

Those preparing for the feud never omit to first consult the spirits, who will let them know whether in the planned attack they will be successful or not. This divination, as already mentioned, is carried out through drinking the narcotic *maikoa*. The Indian for this purpose retires to the forest, where he remains for three days and three nights, fasting strictly and sleeping in a small " dreaming ranch " (*ayámdai*). If the dreams are good, among other spirits the demons, known under the name of *arútama*, appear to the warrior, speaking to him and telling him whether he will be able to kill the enemy or whether he will perhaps be killed himself. " That sorcerer who has bewitched your father you will conquer and kill." Or they say: " If you make war against that sorcerer now, you will not succeed in killing him, but you will be killed yourself." In the latter case the avenger desists from his plan, at least for the present. Again, if the answer is favorable, he with his followers make the last preparations for the attack.

Such an attack is sometimes planned and carried out in greatest secrecy. Sometimes, and more frequently, the victim is threatened beforehand, the avenger letting him know what fate is awaiting him. He may then save himself by quickly flying to another part of the country. But it also happens that he sends his enemies the following menacing challenge: " I have been told that you intend to assault and kill me. All right; you may come if you have valor. I do not fear you, and I am ready to receive you." Such a resolute behavior may cause the enemy to desist from the planned attack or to postpone it to another more opportune time. Among the Jibaros there also exists the following custom, through which the Indians try to inspire the enemy they want to kill with fear. Of a piece of manioc a likeness of a human head in miniature is formed, which is supposed to represent the enemy threatened. This head is put on the top of a stick, and the stick is fixed in the ground in the neighborhood of the enemy's house. This procedure is supposed to have some power of promoting the plans of the avenger.

The conspirators prepare for the assault first by performing that war dance or exercise with the lance which is called *enéma* or *anekma* (in Quichua *tungúni*), and which will be described in connection with the real wars. The *enéma* takes place every night during the last week before the attack is made. The warriors drink much manioc beer to get strength and smoke much tobacco, partly to acquire strength and resistance, partly to ward off evil supernatural influences. On the eve of the day of making the attack they paint their face, breast, arms, and legs black with genipa (in Jibaro called *sua*, in Quichua *huituc*).

The attack is carried out in different ways, depending on the circumstances. Sometimes the victim is attacked in his house at night, sometimes while he is working outside or traveling. In the former case the assault is made a little before dawn, at 4 or 5 o'clock in the morning. The Jibaros begin their day very early, and the family father is the first who gets up. Since it is difficult or impossible to force the entrance, the enemies generally avail themselves of the opportunity when he opens the door to perform his necessary duties. At this moment they rush upon him and kill him with their lances. If they are armed with guns or rifles and the house is not especially fortified they creep along to the wall and through a parting in it try to give the sorcerer the death-dealing shot while he is sitting at the fire preparing his tobacco water or his guayusa. Having accomplished the deed, the assassins quickly steal away, leaving the rest of the inhabitants of the house unmolested.

It is, however, easier to kill the enemy while he is outside the house, working or occasionally wandering in the forest. The conspirators beforehand carefully inquire about the movements of the intended victim, and ambush at a place along the path where he has to pass. This place is generally one where appears some natural obstacle, consisting of a small rivulet which the sorcerer has to wade across, or of a swamp where he is obliged to go slowly. Sometimes they also put up along the path some of the secret signs which the Jibaros use as road marks, or to give friends indications as to the direction they ought to take. When the sorcerer arrives here, he stops to examine what the mark means. At this moment the enemies rush forward and pierce him with their lances or shoot him to death. The dead body is left lying on the path or is thrown into the forest.

It, of course, also occurs that the sorcerer is able successfully to defend himself, nay, even to kill his assailants. The sorcerers are nearly always warriors at the same time—a fact quite natural on account of the danger of their profession—and always go armed, one threatened by his enemies, of course, being especially on the alert.

On the return from such a feud the avengers have for some time to observe certain rules of precaution with regard to their mode of life. The restrictions laid upon them are, however, much milder than those a Jibaro has to observe after he has killed an enemy of a foreign tribe, and essentially consist in fasting and sexual abstinence. During the two first days the slayer or slayers must abstain from drinking manioc beer (*nihamánchi*), the national beverage of the Jibaro Indians. His food consists of boiled and mashed manioc, a dish called *nauma*, or of another kind of root fruit resembling the manioc, called *sangu* by the Jibaros and *mandi* in the Quichua language. He likewise eats a dish prepared of manioc and the leaves of the plant *sangu*, called *ambi*. He is forbidden to eat pork and chicken, as well as the flesh of the large wild hog (*unta pakki*), and of any kind of monkey. On the other hand, he is allowed to eat the small peccary (*yankipi*) and the small rodent agouti (*kayúka*). He eats only the small birds of the forest which are killed with blowpipe and nonpoisoned arrows. He eats only the smallest kinds of fish existing in the rivers, sardines, and small shellfishes (*chumakaí sháchma*). This diet is continued for two or three months. During the first month after having killed the sorcerer the Jibaro is likewise forbidden to sleep in his house, and passes his nights in a small ranch made on the bank of the river. After the lapse of the month he goes to a natural small waterfall (*paccha* or *sasa*) and takes a cold bath, letting the water fall on his naked body. After this purification he returns to his home and may sleep in his house, not with his wife but in the fore-room or department of the men (called *tangámasha*). This sexual abstinence is observed as long as the fasting, namely, for two, or, among some Jibaros, three months. If the rules mentioned are infringed by the slayer the soul of the killed enemy, who constantly follows him thirsting for revenge, will take his life.

Whereas this blood revenge within the tribe is most often carried out simply through assassinations, the feuds fought out between the different tribes are naturally on a larger scale and with more reason deserve the name of " wars." In all his feuds, however, the Indian, if possible, avoids open fights, having recourse to treachery, assassinations, and sudden, generally night, attacks. But if a real combat and hand-to-hand fighting ensue, the Jibaro warrior (pl. 4, *b*) often displays both valor and contempt of death, a fact that is fully proved by the history of the Indians. Not to take flight, not to abandon his comrades in such a situation, but gallantly to meet the enemy with lance and shield, is the ambition of every real Jibaro warrior, and, as we have seen, the education of the boys from the beginning aims at imparting to them the qualities necessary for such behavior.

The general expression of the Jibaros for a war, and more particularly one that is fought out against a foreign tribe, is *meséta*, and to make war means *nanki hukitinyu*, literally "to carry lance for the combat."

When a whole tribe, or eventually several tribes in union, prepare a war against one or more other tribes, the first thing done is to elect a common chief. He should be an elderly, experienced man, who has taken part in several wars, killed many enemies, and celebrated at least one *tsantsa* feast. The rest of the warriors, who are generally younger men, swear him unlimited obedience. During the time the expedition is planned and the preparations are made, the warriors, and especially the chief, repeatedly drink *maikoa* or *natéma* to consult the spirits. They pay great attention to their dreams, even to those not produced under the direct influence of the narcotic drinks; tell them to each other, and discuss their possible significations. Only in case they believe that they have received favorable answers and all omens are good are measures taken to carry out the war plan conceived. Meanwhile they try, through spies, to acquire as accurate a knowledge as possible about everything concerning the enemy: how many houses there are in the tract, how many fighting men in each house, if the houses are fortified, if the men are well armed, and especially if they have firearms. All these and similar details the spies investigate by making trips into the country of the enemy and by stealing at night to the houses. Everything is prepared with the greatest secrecy possible, so that the enemy is caught unprepared, for otherwise he will have time to take measures of defense that may defeat the whole undertaking.

About a week before the warriors start for the expedition they assemble every night in the house of the chief, who develops the plan of the war, gives his men the necessary instructions, exhorts them to take courage, not to fear the enemy, not to abandon their comrades, etc. Part of these instructions are given during the war dance or exercise with the lance, which is called *enéma* or *anekma* (the corresponding verb is *enemártinyu* or *anekmáktinyu*). *Enéma* is a dialogue between two warriors, who through certain movements of the body, and especially of their lances, give emphasis to their words. *Enéma* with the lance (or with a rifle) takes place not only as a preparation for a war, but also, for instance, when two Indians, who are unknown to each other, suddenly meet while traveling in the forest (pl. 5, *a*), or when unknown guests arrive at a house. The one party then has to find out who the newcomer is, if he comes as an enemy or as a friend, from where he comes, where he is going, what business he pursues, etc. The conversation all through has a ceremonial character, and menacing movements with the lance accompany each word or phrase.

The dialogue at the *enéma* is rather stereotyped, the words being always about the same and being repeated several times. The fol-

b. The priest, assisted by some other men, roasting the manioc

a. Jibaro warriors engaged in the ceremonial salutation

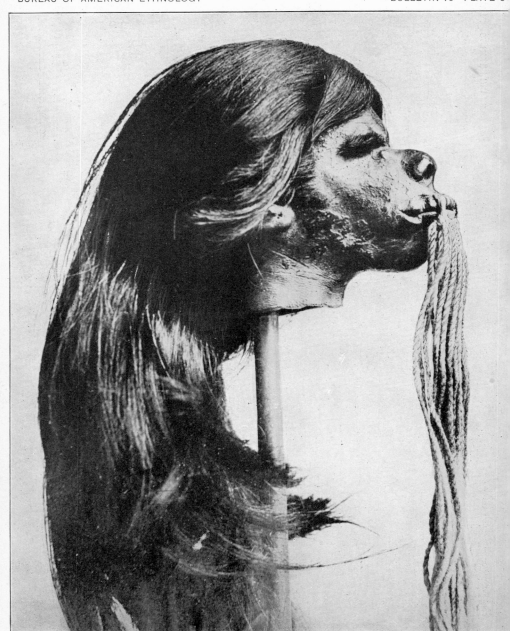

A HUMAN HEAD TROPHY (TSANTSA)

lowing is the *enéma* conversation among the tribes of the Upano, Morona, and Pastaza:

Enemartahei, Let us speak loudly!

Chichama hustai, Let us speak words!

Warita kunai, What are we going to say?

Waru irurtai, Let us quickly assemble!

Tumashi akerkatai, Let us avenge the blood-guilt!

Kashini kanartai, To-morrow we will sleep far away.

Waru nikápsatai, Let us quickly take our enemy!

Waru, chichamahuomo, Quickly, before he is told about it!

Unta nu, So says the Old One (the chief).

Waru wakitketai, uchitai, Let us go, to return quickly, youths!

Huomokki, huomokki, Quickly, quickly!

Manyáhei, We have been fighting!

Mahei, We have killed!

Tumashi ayambruamákahei, We have revenged the blood.

Muka tsupiktai, Let us cut off the head (of the enemy)!

Hukitai, Let us carry it with us.

Enemártinyu (*enemártahei*) means "to speak in a loud voice," which is consistent with the fact that the Indians do not speak in an ordinary voice but shout while carrying out the *enéma* conversation. Each phrase is strongly contracted in the pronunciation, so as to consist only of two to four syllables, which naturally makes the conversation entirely unintelligible to one who does not know the words. In return, the phrase thus contracted is repeated twice, corresponding to the movements of the body. Thus, for instance, the beginning of the conversation:

Chichama hustai,

Warita kunai,

Waru irurtai, etc.

turns out as follows:

Chamurstai chamursti,

Waritkunai waritkuni,

Warurtai warurti,

and so on.

At the beginning of the conversation the two warriors face each other, each having the lance resting on the right shoulder. They speak by turn. The Indian speaking pronounces the phrase in a loud voice, holding the hand over the mouth. With the right arm, upon which the lance rests, he simultaneously makes a movement as if to give emphasis to the words, but he does not, in the beginning, swing the lance and does not move from the spot. Again, in the second repetition or the latter part of the conversation the following movement takes place. The Indian who has the word takes one step toward his opponent, beginning with the left foot, simultaneously raises the right arm with the lance and lets it fall vibrating down on the shoulder; immediately thereafter he goes back to the original position, at the same time again swinging the lance over his shoulder. This whole series of movements is performed quickly and at one time, accompanying the phrase pronounced: *chamurstai chamursti*, etc. One of the conversing Indians having several times repeated this movement with its corresponding phrases, he stops and stands still, the other one then speaking. The whole *enéma* conversation lasts about 15 minutes.

When a war expedition is prepared in which many Indians take part, *enéma* is performed on a large scale. The warriors arrange themselves in two rows, one against the other, so that at the ceremony they converse two and two. If their number is, for instance, 40, 20 are arranged in each row. *Enéma* is then performed simultaneously by all warriors of one row while those of the opposite row stand still with the lances on their shoulders, accompanying the movements and words of the other party with slight gestures of the arms. Having performed the *enéma* for some minutes, the men of the first row keep silence and those of the second row speak, etc.

The *enéma* conversation, as we have seen, implies a mutual exhortation for war and the future course of the combat is passed through, whereat naturally a successful issue of it is anticipated. It is clear that we are not here dealing with an ordinary exercise with the arms. The whole thing is a magical ceremony by which the Jibaros believe themselves to be able to conjure forth victory over the enemy. By making *enéma* the Jibaro warrior is supposed to get strength, courage, and confidence for the coming fight. The war dance is, moreover, believed to enable him to escape the lances and bullets of the enemy in the combat. Besides, the enemy himself is thereby lulled into security so that he will not be aware of the danger threatening, but will be surprised by the assailants. Without *enéma* preparation no war expedition is believed to result favorably. Hence, also, when a house is assaulted by enemies at night, its defenders hurry to make *enéma* with each other before they go to meet the intruding enemy.

About 1 o'clock in the night, when the new day is supposed to begin, the warriors assembled in the house of the chief start to perform *enéma*, which they continue until the break of day. This is repeated every night during one week.

Besides this war dance, the Jibaros try to secure victory over the enemy through a kind of war song. This war song, which is called *anéndrata*, is sung by the warriors in the house before they start for the expedition.

The *anéndrata* runs as follows:

Yachuta, yachuta, My brother, my brother,
Meseta himersatai, Let us make war together!
Winya uchiruna chichahei, To my son also I have said:
Uchita, uchita, My son, my son,
Kákarum hasti, kákarum hasti, Make you strong, make you brave!
Winyaka mástinyu, Me they won't kill.
Wika misérchatinyu, I will not die!
Shuára mákatahei, Myself I will kill my enemy!
Kànárahei, kànárahei, I have dreamed and my dreams have been good.
Arútama weinikama, I have seen "the Old Ones!"[1]
Shuára achiktahei, I will take my enemy.
Yamai achikahei, I have him already!
Mányasa puhústahei, Presently I will be engaged in fighting!
Watski, shuárasha winiti, winiti, All right, may my enemy come, may he come!
Winyasha mandoáti, And may he take my life if he can!
Winya mandoáma assa, If he kills me.
Uchi weinikati, My sons will certainly see (that it will be re-venged).
Chikichika máti, May he kill some one else!

Anéndrata has much the same magical significance as the war dance *enéma,* it being believed to give victory over the enemy.

The warriors, moreover, prepare for the expedition by drinking much manioc beer (*nihamánchi*), as they do for all big travels, without, however, getting too drunk. They likewise take much tobacco, partly in the form of tobacco water, which is drawn in through the nose, partly in the form of cigars, which are smoked.

The preparations of the men take place in the large fore room of the house (*tangámasha*). The women the whole time remain in the interior department (department of the women, *ekínturu*) and do not mix in the activities of the men. The Jibaros on the Upano told me they do not even take leave of their wives before they start for the expedition. If the chief has a wife who is particularly attached to him she may, however, come out, embrace her husband, weeping, and say: "Perhaps you will be killed by the enemy and never return." The chief then consoles her, saying, "I have had good dreams; I won't be killed, but will return with the heads of my enemies. Meanwhile stay you here, quietly making clay vessels."[2]

---

[1] "The Old Ones" (*arútama*), the spirits of the ancestors, who appear to the warrior in the narcotic sleep and tell him that he will be able to kill his enemies.

[2] As if she were already making preparations for the coming victory feasts. The fabrication of clay vessels is the principal preparation of the women for all feasts.

The Jibaro chief Nayapi, on the Rio Pastaza, told me that among his people the warrior starting for an expedition takes tender leave of his wife, embracing her and consoling her, but at the same time preparing her for the eventuality that he, perhaps, will never return and never see her again.

Among the Jibaros of the Pastaza it is also customary for the women during the whole time the men are absent on the warpath to assemble every night in one house and perform a special dance with rattles of snail shells around the waist and chanting conjurations. This war dance of the women, which is called *ihiámbrama*, is supposed to have the power of protecting their fathers, husbands, and sons against the lances and bullets of the enemy, of lulling the latter into security so that he will not apprehend the danger before it is too late, and lastly of preventing him from taking revenge (*ayambruamák-tinyu*) for the defeat inflicted upon him. The dance *ihiámbrama* thus has much the same magical significance as the war dance *enéma* and the war song *anéndrata*.

The warriors march from the house of the chief in a single row, going one after the other, and strictly observing silence. The chief goes out last and shuts the door. During the whole journey to the scene of the war, a journey that takes several days, sometimes even weeks, the warriors are allowed to speak only when necessary, and even then not in a loud voice but in a whisper. Only the chief has the right to speak in a loud voice when at the camping places he gives his men the necessary instructions. As soon as the warriors arrive at the place where they propose to camp that night they arrange themselves in two rows, keeping silence. The chief walks along the rows and gives his instructions, exposes the details of the attack planned and, above all, tries to dispel fear of the young warriors and to inspire them with courage. Although on the march to the war the chief no longer drinks *maikoa* or *natéma*, he still pays great attention to his dreams and from them tries to derive favorable presages. Thus he may with the following words try to inspire his people with courage and confidence: " Take courage and don't fear, for I dreamed this night that I saw the great eagle (*unta pinchu*) and the toucan (*tsukanga*). They told me that we are going to take a *wakáni* (a soul). You are not going to die; you are going to be victors and to kill your enemies."

On the eve of the day fixed for the attack the warriors arrange their dress. The Jibaro always pays great attention to his dress and his ornaments, which form a part of his personality, and at the feasts the dressing has a ceremonial character. The dress of the Jibaro Indian normally consists of a loin cloth (*itipi*) which is attached to the waist by means of a cincture of human hair (*akáchu*), and of another small square cloth, called *awangéama*, which covers the shoulders, with a hole in the middle to pass the head through. The long hair, which is carefully washed and attended every day, is divided into three pigtails, a large one at the neck and two small ones at the temples. In the ears the Jibaro always carries ear tubes (*arusa*) 20 to 30 centimeters long, the ends of which are frequently ornamented with incised figures.

When the Jibaro warrior prepares for an attack against an enemy he puts on his head a sort of cap made of monkey's skin, which he prefers to the ordinary head ornament made of parrot or toucan feathers (*tawása*). The ear tubes ought to be as large as possible so that their ends nearly reach the shoulders. Around the neck the warrior wears a necklace of jaguar's teeth and around the waist the usual cincture of human hair (*akáchu*). Old warriors, however, for an attack prefer to cincture themselves with a broad belt of skin of the great boa. The uncovered part of the body, the face, the breast, the back, the arms, and legs, are finally painted black with genipa (*sua*).

The hair is, as always, divided into the three pigtails mentioned, the latter being tied around with broad bands adorned with toucan feathers and human hair, or with cotton strings which are dyed red with *achiote*. The Jibaros on the Pastaza and the Canelos Indians, for a battle, are in the habit of tying around the pigtails or the hair broad basten strips obtained from a plant which the former call *chipyata*, the latter *chilipanga*. These basten strips, which are of bright colors, are partly used as signs by which the warriors, in the darkness and in the heat of battle, are able to distinguish friends from foes, and are also worn because of some mysterious power ascribed to them or to the plant from which they are taken.

With regard to the arrangement of the dress for war there are three objects which are kept in view. Partly, the Indian tries to make his whole appearance as terrifying as possible in order to impress the enemies; partly, certain pieces of clothing and ornaments which he puts on are, owing to some mysterious inherent properties, supposed to give him strength and courage; lastly, some of them will serve as marks of recognition, by which the warriors will be able to distinguish friends from enemies in the battle. The black body painting, for instance, serves all these three aims. It, more than anything else, contributes to giving the Indian warrior a savage and terrible appearance. The Jibaros say that for a combat they paint themselves black in order to resemble the *iguanchi* (demons), which implies that the body painting is believed to impart to them something of the savage ferocity and strength of these supernatural beings. Besides, even in semidarkness it is possible to distinguish the black-painted Indian from one who does not wear that mark of recognition. The basten strips tied around the pigtails likewise, as already indicated, partly

enable the warriors to recognize their comrades in the battle, partly
are supposed to eke out that natural power which the Indian always
ascribes to his hair and his pigtails. To impart strength and valor
to the warrior is also the object of the ear tubes, the necklaces of
jaguar's teeth, and the belt of the boa serpent. "Wearing our ear
tubes (*arúsa*), we do not fear anything," the Jíbaros are in the habit
of saying. The teeth of the jaguar and the belt of the boa skin naturally give the wearer something of the demoniac strength of these
animals. Again, the power which the Jíbaros attribute to the cincture
made of human hair depends on the supernatural properties ascribed
to the hair, which is regarded as the seat of the soul or the vital en
ergy.

Having arrived at the tract inhabited by the hostile tribe the warriors, if possible, try to surprise and kill particular persons belonging to the tribe, who, unaware of the danger, happen to be outside
the houses, working in the plantations or walking in the forest. The
proper attacks are, however, according to the general custom of the
Indians, made at night or early in the morning, a little before dawn.
Keeping strict silence, the enemies surround the house on all sides
and ambush in the immediate neighborhood of it, expecting that
someone will go out and open the door. That person is then in-
stantly killed by a lance or a rifle shot, whereupon the enemies speedily penetrate into the house and massacre the rest of its inhabitants.
In case it proves impossible to penetrate into the house by treachery,
the enemies set fire to it by firebrands thrown upon its roofing, oblig-
ing the inhabitants to leave it and killing them during the confusion
that follows. If in this way the assailants have been able to kill all
the people in one house, and there is no fear of other Indians coming
to the rescue, they may go to the next house and continue the massacre, for, as already pointed out, the wars carried out against foreign
tribes always aim at completely exterminating the enemy if possible.

However, the enemy is not always in this way surprised and unprepared, and is not always annihilated without resistance. Thus
the measures of defense, described above, may, at least to a certain
extent, frustrate the plans of the attacking party.

Not seldom the inhabitants of the house, through the dogs and the
chickens, or in some other way, get knowledge of the presence of the
enemy, and the latter may then to his disappointment suddenly hear
the beats of the great signal drums in the fast time which is a sure
sign for the friends that the people of the house are in danger. The
assailants then have to choose between quickly retiring or pursuing
the attack and engaging in a fight the result of which, owing to the
help eventually arriving, is uncertain.

However, if the enemy has already surrounded the house, there
is little hope for those shut up in it to be saved through the inter-

vention of friends. Their possibility of salvation then consists almost solely in breaking through the besieging ring and speedily flee-
ing to another house or into the forest. Before making this desper-
ate attempt, however, all inhabitants of the house, men, women, and
children, assemble to perform, in haste, a dance, *hantsēmata*. Holding each other by the hands they move in a circle in the house in the
way customary at most Indian dances, chanting or making noise and
playing a set of flutes made of the leg bone of the jaguar, called
tungüi. The words uttered, or rather shouted, are the following:

Māsteitimi, They won't kill us!

Mandoástatami, They won't take our lives!

Wuittatai, They will retire!

Hīnikitai, We will be able to escape!

The object of this ceremony is to "tire out the enemy" (*shuāra
pimbíktinyu*), so that he gives up the plan of attacking the house and
retires. Sometimes it also occurs that the besieging enemies, who,
of course, understand what the dancing and shouting in the house
mean, lose courage, give up the plan of attack, and draw off.

Immediately after the dance mentioned has been performed the
inhabitants of the house try to escape through one or both of its
doors. As soon as the ambushing enemies notice this they incite each
other with cries:

Shuāra hīniwui, The enemy leaves the house!

Awuímaipa, Don't let them escape!

Ihúta, ihúta, ihúta, Lance them, lance them!

During the fight ensuing it may happen that some, or the majority, of the people in the house are able to save themselves in the
darkness and the confusion. Generally, however, some old man or
some women, who are not able to run quickly enough, get into the
hands of the pursuing enemy, being killed or captured. If the victors
are satisfied with this spoil, or if for one reason or another they do
not venture to continue the persecution, they speedily return, carrying with them one or more heads which they have cut off or some
captured woman, and giving triumphant war cries:

Hetéktatai, May they now pursue us!

Aimiayáhei, Now we carry off their comrade!

Yúhi, uyúhi, uyúhi!

Tuo, tuo, tuo! (War cries.)

It is, however, only in case the attacked people have been surprised
unprepared and know they are absolutely inferior to the enemy that
they try in this way to save themselves by flight. In other cases it
happens that the attacking enemy is received by a number of well-
prepared and well-armed warriors who, after having in a hurry performed the *enéma*, gallantly go out to meet the assailants. A fierce

hand-to-hand fight then ensues, in which friends and enemies mix with each other in the darkness, and the noise of arms is drowned by the inciting war cries of the men, by the cries of the women and the children, and by the barking of the dogs.

The victorious enemy without mercy wreaks his savage vengeance not only upon the fighting men, but also on old people, women, and small children, nay, sometimes even on the domestic animals. The younger women are, however, often spared and carried off as prisoners of war, their fate being later to add to the number of their victors', and especially the chief's, wives. There are also numerous instances of small children being spared to be brought up as members of the victorious tribe. For the rest, the Indian does not content himself with merely killing his enemy. He wants to shed as much blood as possible and delights in mutilating the body of the slain enemy, being especially anxious to secure his head. The scene of a battle between Jibaro Indians, therefore, generally appears a dreadful spectacle of savage lust of destruction and thirst for blood.

The lance, a terrible weapon of the Jibaros, inspires not only living men but even the spirits and demons with fear. The soul of an Indian killed with the lance in terror flees far away from the mutilated body and does not remain for some time in the neighborhood, as is believed to be the case at ordinary death. The relatives themselves stand in such horror of the dead body that they only hurriedly bury it on the same spot where they find it, thereafter speedily leaving the place. The devoted cult which the Jibaros generally pay to their dead relatives entirely fails with regard to those killed in war, and food is never put on their graves.

THE HEAD TROPHY (TSANTSA) AND ITS PREPARATION

As pointed out before, the Jibaros never make trophies (pl. 6) of the heads of such enemies as belong to their own tribe; that is, with whom they reckon blood relationship. An Indian who did this would run the risk of being himself killed by his tribesmen, even by those neutral before. On the other hand, it is the rule that when a victory has been attained over a foreign tribe, the heads of the slain enemies are taken. Most Jibaro warriors would consider any victory over such an enemy incomplete, and the whole war expedition more or less a failure, unless they returned with one or several head trophies. It, of course, not seldom happens that the Jibaro is able to kill an enemy but not to take his head, because his comrades are able to secure the dead body and perhaps to defeat the slayers. In such a case there can not be a real victory feast. It occurs, however, sometimes, that an enthusiastic Jibaro warrior invites his friends and celebrates a small feast, consisting in drinking bouts and dancing, although he has not been able to capture a trophy but only to kill his enemy.

Contrariwise, it may happen in exceptional cases that a Jibaro, although he has acquired a trophy, does not care to celebrate a feast with it, either because he considers himself too poor to procure the great supply of food necessary for the many guests at such a feast or because he has not enough people in his house to prepare it or friends to invite to it. Thus the great Jibaro chief Nayapi, of Pastaza, has killed about 20 enemies, but has not celebrated a single *tsantsa* feast, evidently in part because his many enemies have not given him the peace and tranquillity necessary for preparing such a feast.

The rule is, however, among the Jibaros that a warrior who has captured a head (*tsantsa*) should celebrate a feast. The head feast for the Jibaro opens the road to honor and fame, to material wealth, to new victories over enemies, and a long life. It is the great mystery feast of the Jibaro Indians; as will presently be seen, it in part has a purely religious significance, inasmuch as the Jibaro through the ceremonies thereby performed believes he acquires the same benefits as most other savage peoples try to acquire by cult actions of different kinds.

As soon as a Jibaro warrior has killed an enemy of another tribe he at once tries to secure his head, which he cuts off as close to the trunk as possible. The warrior who has cut off the head (*muka tsupikma*) is the "lord of the head" (*muka heindinyu*) and the first who, when the victors are many, has the right to celebrate a feast with it. When several Indians in union have killed one enemy it is customary for each of them in turn to celebrate a victory feast with the trophy, which in this case is taken from one house to another.

During the speedy return which generally follows upon a successful attack there is not always time for the victors to at once begin with the preparation of the trophy. They at first have to put themselves in safety from the eventually pursuing enemy. Thus it occurs that they carry the bloody head with them during a couple of days before they get an opportunity to "skin" it (*muka sukurtinyu*). In this work only those warriors engage who have taken part in the killing of the enemy. If the victors are many, and they have been able to acquire only one head, it happens that some of them separate themselves from the rest, saying: "We go off to kill other enemies and to capture our own heads."

Those who remain now start to take off the scalp from the head. At first the following small ceremony takes place: The head is placed upon a large leaf on the ground. Upon the head there is placed another leaf of the forest which the Jibaros call *pingi nuka*, and to which certain magical virtues are ascribed. The warrior who cuts off the head now seats himself on this "seat" and receives juice of tobacco mixed with saliva from the chief, who blows it in through his nose. Then another of the slayers takes his seat on the head and receives juice of tobacco through the nose, etc., until all have partaken. This is the first of a series of ceremonies which have for their object the protection of the slayers against the revengeful spirit of the killed enemy.

The *tsantsa* is now prepared in the following way: Along the back side of the head, from the apex downward, a long cut is made with a knife, whereupon the scalp and the skin of the face is slowly and carefully drawn off from the skull, in much the same way as is done with the hides of animals for stuffing. The skinning of the face is said to be the most difficult part of this work, for here the skin does not loosen by merely drawing it off, but has to be cut from the flesh with a sharp knife. The skull and all fleshy parts that adhere to it are thrown away and the scalp obtained is further prepared. It is attached to a vine and immersed in a pot of boiling water, where it is left for a while. By boiling the scalp it is freed from microbes, contracts a little, and gets more consistence. It is then taken out of the pot and put on the top of a stick, fixed in the ground, where it is left for a while until it has cooled.

A ring is formed of a vine which the Jibaros call *câpi*, of the same size as the circumference of the ready-made *tsantsa* at the neck opening, and this ring is attached to the trophy, at first provisionally, and later, in the same degree as the latter assumes its final size through reduction, more firmly. By means of a needle and a thread consisting of a chambira fiber, that part of the scalp which, for the purpose of the skinning of the head, had been cut open, is sewn together.

The reduction of the trophy now should begin. What at first is done with it, however, rather has the character of some sort of magical ceremony. At the bank of the river three small round stones are looked for, which are heated at the fire. By means of a cleft stick one of the heated stones is taken up from the fire and put into the head through the opening at the neck. This is done by the first slayer (he who cuts off the head of the enemy), whose hand is held by the chief or an old warrior. The head is kept in motion so that the heated stone rolls to and fro within it, burning off a part of the blood and flesh which is still attached to the scalp. The stone is subsequently taken out and again put in the fire. The same procedure is repeated with the second stone, and lastly with the third stone. The stones used are each time put back on the fire, where they are left.

Since a similar procedure is afterwards undertaken with heated sand, the use of the three small stones seems somewhat superfluous.

Probably the object of this treatment is only to mortify the soul of the killed enemy, attached to the scalp, and to keep it at bay. This explanation is made more probable by the fact that the ceremony with the three stones is repeated later, at the great feast, and obviously without practical aim.

The proper reduction of the trophy is brought about by means of hot sand. Some fine sand is taken from the river bank and heated at the fire in a piece of broken clay pot (*hakáchi*). When the sand is sufficiently hot it is poured into the head so as to more than half fill it. The head is kept in motion so that the sand acts uniformly upon all its parts. The object of this procedure is to remove the flesh still attached to the skin, to make the scalp thinner, and to reduce the whole trophy. This is attained by the procedure with the hot sand being repeated many times. As soon as the sand has cooled it is taken out of the head, reheated at the fire in the broken clay pot, and again poured into the head. Each time, after taking out the sand from the head, the scalp is scraped inside with a knife in order to remove from it what the sand has burned off. As the trophy dries and shrinks through this treatment the head, and especially the face, is cleverly molded with the fingers, so that it retains its human features, becoming like the head of a small dwarf. This work is continued during the whole return from the war, eventually even at home, consequently during several days or even weeks, the same sand and the same broken clay vessel being always used. These things are always kept and carried on the march by the first slayer, whose duty it is, as soon as the party arrives at a camping place, to collocate the clay pot on the fire and heat sand for the molding of the trophy.

It is considered necessary that the sand shall be heated in an old broken clay pot. An entire clay vessel, or a piece of a quite new clay vessel, would not do.

By this treatment the Jibaros are able to gradually reduce the head to such an extent that it is no larger than an orange, or about one-fourth of its normal size, becoming at the same time completely hard and dry. Through both lips, shrunk in proportion to the rest of the head, three small chonta pins, about 5 centimeters in length and painted red with *achiote*, are passed parallel with each other, and around these pins a fine cotton string, which is also painted red, is wound. At the great feast both the chonta pins and the cotton string are removed and replaced by three twined and red-painted cotton strings. Lastly the whole trophy, even the face, is dyed black with charcoal (pl. 6).

During the whole work particular attention has been paid to the hair, which is the most essential part of the trophy. Among the Jibaros the men as a rule wear their hair much longer than the women, and *tsantsas* with hair half a meter or more long are therefore not uncommon. The hair, according to the idea of the Indians, is the seat of the soul or the vital power.

Since the *tsantsa* itself is an object charged with supernatural power, it is intelligible that many arrangements at its preparation are of a magical nature or depend on superstitious ideas of one kind or another. This holds good, for instance, of the ceremony with the three heated stones, described before. Likewise, the arrangement with the red-painted chonta pins, with which the lips are pierced, and the red cotton string wound round them, as well as the blackening of the trophy, do not serve any reasonable practical purpose, but must be set down to pure superstition. The Jibaros themselves, who mostly try to give as natural an explanation of their strange practices as possible, say that the chonta pins are applied with a view to keeping the mouth of the trophy closed, and that the red-painted cotton string is merely a decoration. Since, however, the Indians ascribe a special mysterious power to the hardwood of the spring chonta palm—a power further increased through the red paint—and red-painted cotton string likewise plays a part in their superstitious practices, it is more than probable that the real aim of the ornaments mentioned is to keep the soul of the murdered enemy under a constant magical force, perhaps also to paralyze the curses proceeding from the mouth of the victim. With the same view the *tsantsa* is at the feast generally held tied to a lance of chonta.

The preparation of the head trophy requires great skill and care, for through some slight carelessness, for instance, at the removal of the scalp, or at the burning, the whole thing may easily be entirely spoiled. The young Jibaro who has killed an enemy for the first time is therefore instructed in its preparation by an older warrior. Nor can an Indian prepare the head alone. Hence, when a Jibaro warrior has killed an enemy alone and taken his head he needs the help of another man, at least for the skinning of the head. This assistant necessarily ought to be a warrior who likewise has earlier killed some enemy. Another Indian would not have " a good hand " for the work and would not do.

The stronger the killed enemy had been in life, the more valiantly he had fought, the more difficult it had been to deprive him of life, the greater is the honor the victor earns by his deed, the greater is the power of the trophy made of his head. Notwithstanding this, it sometimes occurs among the Jibaros that *tsantsas* are prepared even of heads of women.

But the Jibaro Indian does not make trophies solely of the heads of his human enemies but also of the heads of certain animals. There is one animal especially which in this respect plays a curious part in the superstitions of the Jibaros, namely, the sloth, called *uyúshi* by them. Feasts with trophies made of the head of the sloth are among the Jibaros equally common as feasts with human *tsantsas*. This fact derives its explanation from the mythology of these Indians. In primitive times, the Jibaros tell, all animals—quadrupeds, birds, fishes, reptiles, and so on—were men, i. e., Jibaros. They had human shape, human habits, human thoughts and passions, and human language. They also waged wars against each other, and made trophies of the heads of their slain enemies, just as the Jibaros still do. Later on this kind of folk were changed into animals, the animals which still exist. The Jibaros still have a very vivid consciousness of their supposed relationship with the animal world, a feature which especially appears in their religion and their poetry. But they especially claim to trace the ancient human qualities in the sloth. This helpless animal, according to their idea, is a direct survival from the remote period mentioned. It is still a Jibaro in the shape of an animal, but a Jibaro of a foreign tribe and consequently an enemy. He is a very old man, as one may judge from his slow movements and from the fact that his hair is partly gray.[3] The Jibaros even profess to know what his name was in ancient times, while a man. He was then called *Unúpi*, his wife's name was *Unuchi*, and his brother's *Uyungra*. When, therefore, the Jibaros meet a sloth, they kill it with a lance, just as they kill their human enemies, and make a trophy of its head. This trophy is prepared in the same way as a human *tsantsa*, but is only reduced a little, since the head of the sloth is comparatively small. In the trophy made of the sloth the fell of the neck corresponds to the hair of a human *tsantsa*. The fell of that part is therefore conserved and prepared with care. The Indian who has killed the animal has thereafter to pass through exactly the same purificatory ceremonies as one who has killed a human enemy, and even the final great victory feast is celebrated in due time with exactly the same grand preparations and with the same carefully performed ceremonies.

There are also instances of trophies having been made by the Jibaros of the head of the jaguar. Many years ago an Indian woman was killed by a jaguar in the neighborhood of Rio Zamora. The Jibaros regard a jaguar, which in this way attacks and kills people, as the incarnation of the soul of an evil sorcerer which has entered that wild beast with a view to harming or killing his enemies. The Indians consequently resolved to take revenge, arranged a hunting

---

[3] The superstition held of the sloth is partly due to the fact that the animal is extremely tenacious of life. This the Jibaros suppose to be the case with old people in general. When the Jibaro warrior has succeeded in killing an enemy who was an old man and whom it was very difficult to deprive of life, he regards the victory as a special triumph.

of the animal, and succeeded in killing it. They thereafter made a trophy of its head, and a victory feast was celebrated in the ordinary way.

As to other rules of precaution which the warriors have to observe after the victory the following may be mentioned: In the evening of the day the enemies have been killed all warriors who have taken part in the massacre slightly prick themselves over the whole body, the arms, legs, shoulders, breast, and stomach with a pointed arrow of the kind the Jibaros use for their blowpipes. This is believed to protect them against the spirit of the killed enemy. In the dream the slayer meets the spirit, who says to him: " Come, let us dance together." The warrior's own soul or spirit then answers: " No; I can not dance, for I have my body full of sores." If in the evening he has not pricked himself in the way mentioned, he will in the dream obey the exhortation of the inimical spirit to dance with him, and the consequence of this will be that the warrior will soon die. The Jibaros therefore say that they prick themselves in the way described " in order not to die."

In regard to the diet of the Jibaro warriors, there is nothing prescribed for the time they are preparing for and marching to the war. They may then eat whatever they like. But as soon as a Jibaro has killed an enemy the fasting begins. All those who took part in the killing of the enemy are, during the return home, allowed to eat only boiled and mashed manioc, a dish called *nauma*. This food has to be cooked exclusively by the slayers themselves. No other man, and still less a woman, may prepare it. When the warriors eat they never touch the manioc with their fingers, like the Jibaros generally do, but they use small wooden pins to eat with. Their hands having been polluted with the blood of their enemies, the food would become impure if they touched it, and they would expose themselves to death.

Moreover, the warriors are not allowed to bathe or to wash themselves in any way until they reach home. Dirty and soiled with blood, as they departed from battle, they should arrive home. This, of course, also holds good for their clothing, their loin cloth (*itipi*) and other clothes, as well as their weapons, the bloody lance with which the enemy was killed, and the knife with which his head was cut off. It is not until later, at the general ceremonial purification at home, that the warrior himself and his weapons can be washed.

Ever since the hour when the warrior killed his enemy, and up to the feast which is called *suamartinyu*, and which is celebrated some months later, he is not either allowed to have sexual intercourse with a woman or even to sleep in the same room with a woman.

NUMBUIMARTINYU, "THE WASHING OF THE BLOOD"

Immediately after their return the victor or victors have to pass through the purification procedure, connected with a small feast, which the Jibaros call *numbuimartinyu* (from *númba*, blood, and *mártinyu*, to paint, to coat), the principal ceremony of which consists in their legs being coated with chicken's blood. If the victors are many, this ceremony is at first performed with the one who cut the head of the enemy, and thereafter by turns with each of those who took part in the killing. Before the victors, who travel slowly and stop in various houses on the way, arrive home, a message has been sent that the warriors are coming, that a head has been captured and that the preparations for the feast *numbuimartinyu* should begin at once. This feast therefore always has a more or less improvised character.

The first slayer stops in the house of some relations in the neighborhood of his home until the trophy is definitely prepared. It is not until then that his solemn entrance into his own house can take place. He is in the dress of a penitent, has his hair untied, and wears no body-painting or other ornaments. At his side stands the chief or some other old warrior, who will lead the ceremonies at the following feasts and in this capacity is called *whuéa*. Behind these two men the rest of the warriors arrange themselves in a row. The *whuéa* at first gives the slayer juice of tobacco through the nose. Thereafter the latter disengages the trophy from the cloth in which it has been enveloped and with the aid of the old man hangs it round his neck, over the breast. Followed by the rest of the men, he now slowly and ceremoniously, and continually smoothing the hair of the trophy with the hand, proceeds toward the house, stopping outside the door. From within all the women come to meet him, arranged in a row and holding each other by the hands, all in festive dresses and with rattles of snail's shells around the cinctures. On each side of the women the men arrange themselves in two rows inside the house. The introductory dance with the trophy which is called *ihiámbrama*, and which is performed by the victor together with the women, now takes place. From among the women two step forth who have been standing at the head of the rest. Those are the wife and daughter of the victor. For the following dance the daughter grasps him from behind at the cincture with both hands; the wife gives him her hand, standing at the head of the other women. The slayer again seizes the *tsantsa* with the right hand, holding it up with the arm stretched out; with the left he grasps the hand of his wife. All now pass, dancing or hopping with the side foremost, into the interior of the house, to the accompaniment of drums and the rattles of the women, and immediately return to the entrance. The same maneuver is repeated twice more. Each time the slayer, led by the women, returns to the entrance of the house. The aim of this dance is to paralyze the danger threatening the victor from the spirit of the murdered enemy at the first entrance into the house, which is regarded as particularly critical.

The slayer now takes off the *tsantsa* and the latter is tied to a chonta lance which is fixed in the ground close to the door at the inner side. The lance must be made of the hard wood of the chonta palm, to which the Indians ascribe a supernatural power. Another kind of lance, for instance one having an iron point, would not do. In this way the *tsantsa* is kept even at the following feasts during the time it is not needed for the ceremonies. The trophy being tied to the chonta lance, the spirit of the enemy attached to it is mortified and kept at bay.

The *whuéa* lays his hand upon the shoulder of the slayer and takes him round in the house as if to manifest that he can now move about there without danger.

Meanwhile, close to the lance with the *tsantsa* tied to it, two small vessels have been placed. One is a piece of an old broken clay pot (*hakáchi*) containing a little chicken's blood, the other an ordinary small pot with a solution of genipa (*sua*). These three objects, the lance with the trophy tied to it, the piece of the clay pot containing chicken's blood, and the small pot with genipa, seem to be sacred; no unauthorized person may touch them or even come near them.

If among the warriors who took part in the killing of the enemy two or more are from the same house, being for instance two brothers or a father with his sons, a special broken clay vessel with chicken's blood and a special small pot with genipa must be placed at the lance for each of them. The ceremony *numbuimartinyu*, thus, must be performed separately with each slayer from the same house.

The "washing of the blood" now takes place. The slayer takes his seat upon a small round bank close to the vessel with the chicken's blood and the *whuéa* places himself at his side. Around them the women form a semicircle, having their rattles around the cincture as before. They are led by an old woman, called *oháha*, who at the feasts directs all those ceremonies at which the women play the main part. The *whuéa* at first gives the slayer juice of tobacco through the nose. Then he grasps him by the hand, brings it down to the vessel containing the chicken's blood, lets him dip the index finger into it, and subsequently with the blood draw a broad line 2 or 3 inches in length along the front side of one of his legs, from beneath upward. Thereafter the slayer, with the aid of the *whuéa*, applies a similar stroke with the blood to his other leg. While this is being done the women, led by the *oháha*, dance in a ring around them, singing a sort of conjuration, which mainly consists of the following phrase:

Whuéa heingi ikäski numbimarmai ihambratinyu; that is, "The *whuéa*, together with the *oháha (ikäski)*, paint you with blood to start the fasting."

As we shall see, the ceremony *numbuimartinyu* introduces a time of very strict fasting for the slayer.

The slayer now in his turn does the *whuéa* the same service, drawing with his index finger two streaks with the chicken's blood upon both his legs.

The blood-painting ceremony having been finished, the piece of broken clay vessel, together with the blood left in it, is immediately thrown away into the forest. It is an impure and harmful substance which need no longer be kept.

The *whuéa* asks the wife of the slayer for water, and she brings it in a clay dish (*pininga*). The old man takes a little water from the dish with his hand and puts it upon the head of the slayer. Thereafter he does the same with the wife and daughter of the slayer, putting with his hand a little water upon their heads. All three are subsequently sent down to the river to bathe.

That even the wife and the daughter of the slayer have to pass through this purification procedure and afterwards also have to take part in various other ceremonies is partly due to the close relationship existing between them and the slayer, but especially to the rôle they have played at the dance *ihiámbrama*. By touching the still bloodstained hands and clothes of the slayer they have likewise been polluted with the blood of the murdered enemy, are consequently exposed to danger from the revengeful spirit, and have to be purified from the blood and observe other rules of precaution. From this moment up to the time for the celebration of the final great victory feast they have thus to fast in the same way as the slayer himself, assisting at the said feast again at the dance *ihiámbrama*, which then will be repeated.

If the slayer has two wives they generally assist at the dance mentioned. If he is quite a young man, who has not yet married, it is considered obligatory that he should look for a bride for the feast. The part of the other woman in this case is played by some near female relative of his.

In the river the slayer carefully washes his whole body, as well as his clothing, soiled with blood in the battle, and lastly his weapons, the still bloody lance and knife. Together with his wife and daughter, who have also washed themselves, he then returns to the house.

On the way they break some twigs of guayusa (*Ilex* sp.), called *weisa* by the Jibaros, a tree the leaves of which are used for the preparation of an aromatic and tonic drink, with which the Jibaros wash their mouths every morning. This drink has now to be prepared. The slayer as well as his wife and daughter together grasp a small clay pot, called *yukúnda*, pour water into it from a larger vessel, and together place it on the fire. As soon as the drink has boiled the *whuéa* takes a little of it in a small gourd, mutters an incantation over it, and passes it to the slayer who washes his mouth with it without swallowing much of it. Thereafter the *whuéa* in the same way gives of the drink to the wife and the daughter of the slayer, who likewise wash their mouths with it. The small clay pot is then taken off the fire and laid aside. The three persons are now properly purified for breaking the fast.

The wife of the slayer goes to fetch the edible top of a small palm which the Jibaros call *tingími*, which is put on the fire to be roasted, exactly on the same place where the guayusa pot had lain. At another fire in the house beans have before been cooked, and at a third manioc, afterwards mashed, a dish called *nauma*. As soon as the palm top is sufficiently roasted the women move over to this fire, take a dish with beans, and another dish with boiled manioc (*nauma*). The three principal persons, the slayer himself and his wife and daughter, now have to break the fast after the " washing of the blood." The *whuéa* at first gives juice of tobacco to the slayer through the nose. Then with two fingers he takes a little of the palm top (*tingími*), spits on the ground, mutters an incantation over it and puts it directly into the mouth of the slayer, who swallows it. Then with two fingers he takes a few beans, and lastly also a small piece of boiled manioc together with a little salt and a little pimiento or Indian pepper, and gives them to the slayer with the same ceremony. Exactly the same action is repeated with his wife and his daughter, each of whom likewise receives a little of the dishes mentioned. The vessels with the food are subsequently carried away by the other women.

Meanwhile food has also been cooked for the guests in the women's department of the house. This food essentially consists of boiled chicken. If there are swine in the house, one is also slaughtered and prepared, but according to old tradition boiled chicken is the main dish at the feast *numbuimartinyu*.

A general banquet now commences, at which the guests eat chicken and manioc, whereas the slayer, his wife, and daughter eat the palm top *tingími*, beans, and manioc.

After the banquet the last ceremony takes place, which consists in the slayer being painted with genipa (*sua*). The slayer seats himself on a bank in front of the pot containing the black dye, and the *whuéa* places himself at his side, grasps his hand, makes him dip his index finger in the solution and apply a broad stroke with it over the mouth so that both lips are painted black. Thereafter the old man draws a similar black stroke over his own mouth. The women simultaneously dance around the two men, singing an incantation. The pot containing the genipa is now carried away and kept.

The *whuéa* at last addresses the slayer with a sort of speech wherein he points out that he himself has now fulfilled his mission to wash off the blood from the slayer, but that the latter has now to prepare himself for the celebration of the final great victory feast. He has to breed swine and chickens to be slaughtered at the feast; he must plant fields of manioc and plantain; he must in his life carefully observe certain rules of abstinence from eating certain kinds of food, etc.

When darkness sets in, or about 6 o'clock in the evening, a general dance commences, which takes place at all great feasts and is called *hantsēmáta*. This dance will be described later in connection with the *tsantsa* feast proper. The slayer himself takes part in the dance with the trophy hanging on his back. It has to be continued during the whole night until dawn. That night no one in the house is allowed to sleep, and especially not the slayer himself.

The aim of the feast *numbuimartinyu*, as already mentioned, is to purify the slayer from the blood which is attached to him after the killing of the enemy, and to protect him against the spirit of the latter, who is thirsting for revenge. In the blood the soul of the enemy is particularly supposed to be present. How this purification can be brought about with the two strokes of blood applied to the legs of the slayer is something the Jibaros can not explain more closely. Nor can they explain why chicken's blood must necessarily be used for this procedure, or why that blood must be kept in an old, broken clay pot. " Our ancestors have since times immemorial proceeded in this way," an old Jibaro, whom I asked about the custom, answered me, "and we have to keep up and follow their customs." That a magical power and supernaturally purifying effects are ascribed to the chicken's blood is, however, clear. The same purifying effects, in a magical or religious sense of the word, are ascribed to the bath in the river and to the washing of the mouth with *guayusa*, the object of the latter ceremony especially being to favorably prepare for the breaking of the fast. Again, the painting with the genipa is a direct protection against the spirit of the enemy. Body painting among the Indians nearly always serves magical ends, being regarded as a protection against disease and witchcraft, and this is especially the case with the black painting. According to the ideas of the Jibaros and the Canelos Indians there is a demon (*wakani, supai*) in the black genipa paint, and when the Indian paints his body or face black this is usually a sign that he either is going to kill an enemy or already has killed one. As we shall see, painting with genipa also takes place at the feast *suamartinyu* and at the final great victory feast.

In regard to the question why the chicken's blood used at the purification ought to be kept in an old broken clay vessel (*hakáchi*) it may be mentioned that the Jibaros make use of broken clay pots at certain cathartic rites, when they try to get rid of something that is impure, detestable, and dangerous. Since the chicken's blood which has purified the slayer afterwards is an impure and harmful matter and accordingly is thrown away at once, it is consonant with ritualistic principles that it should be kept in a useless vessel, worthy of being thrown away, like the piece of a broken clay pot. It seems to be due to similar considerations when the Jibaros use a *hakáchi* for heating the sand with which the trophy is reduced at the preparation.

Again, if one asks what ideas underlie the choice of the slayer's food—palm top, beans, mashed manioc, etc.—the Indians only give the explanation that he ought to eat such light kinds of food that remain in his stomach and which he does not run the risk of throwing up, which evidently would be regarded as dangerous for him. Their idea is, no doubt, that a very indigestible or irritating food could become a means through which the invisible, supernatural enemy of the slayer—the spirit of the killed enemy—could get an opportunity to harm him, perhaps cause his death. That the guests mainly eat chicken at the feast is probably only due to the fact that *numbuimartinyu* is an improvised feast, and that, therefore, such kinds of food is given them as is most easy to procure.

The prescriptions with regard to the diet and mode of life which the slayer has to observe during the time immediately following the " washing of the blood," or up to the feast called *suamartinyu*, which is celebrated some months later, are very severe and strict. He is not even allowed to dress completely, but only wears his loin cloth (*itipi*), tied up with a cincture, having the upper part of the body bare. The hair is generally kept loose and is not arranged in the three pigtails normally worn by the Jibaros. Only at the neck the hair is occasionally tied up. He must not wear ear tubes, facial painting, necklaces, or other ornaments of any kind. He can not carry a lance or other weapon, nor handle poison⁴ or other dangerous matter, nor go out hunting or fishing or on new war expeditions, nor take part in feasts. When the slayer goes out wandering he, instead of the lance without which normally no Jibaro leaves his house, only carries a short staff. He is also prohibited from having sexual intercourse with his wife or even from sleeping in the women's department of the house (*ekinturu*), but passes his nights in the fore room or men's department (*tangámasha*). His diet is the lightest pos-

---

⁴ This prohibition especially touches the arrow poison (*seasa*), and the varvasco poison (*tima*), used in fishing.

sible and consists only of the palm top (*tingimi*), which is eaten roasted, of boiled and mashed manioc (*nauma*), and of the smallest kinds of fish caught in the rivers (sardines, *chumakai*, and another kind of small fish, *sháchma*). These may be boiled or roasted, but must be eaten without addition of other kinds of food.

The wife and daughter of the slayer must also fast. Their food during the period in question consists principally of beans and of the leaves of a forest plant which the Jibaros call *épo*.

If the slayer infringes these rules the consequences for him will be fatal. He will soon die; he will not be able to kill any more enemies or to celebrate other *tsantsa* feasts. Even his nearest relatives will die through sickness or accidents, one after another.[5] His domestic animals, instead of increasing and flourishing, will pine away and die. The manioc, plantain, and other domestic plants will dry away and produce no fruits. In all his undertakings he will be unlucky. In one word, the effects of the trophy will be directly contrary to those generally expected from its supernatural power. All this is caused by the spirit of the murdered enemy (*wakáni*). The revengeful ghost, who takes no rest, follows his slayer everywhere, always looking for an opportunity to kill or harm him, and the latter believes that he meets him especially in dreams. Generally the *wakáni* meets him in the shape of an Indian armed with a lance, with which he is continually trying to kill him. But the spirit also appears to him in other shapes, especially in the shape of a black monkey, a deer,[6] a bear, or some other hairy animal of the forest. This is one of the reasons why the slayer does not, during the critical time, go out wandering in the forest. The *wakáni* can here in many ways threaten his life. If, for instance, he wanders to the verge of a precipice at the bank of a river the revengeful demon may take an opportunity to push him over the precipice. He also may cause a tree or a branch to fall upon him in the forest and crush him. If he wears a lance or a knife the spirit may cause his death with these weapons. If he tries to shoot a bird or an animal with blowpipe and poisoned arrows the enemy may cause the arrow to hit the slayer himself. For the same reason he has to be extremely careful in other respects. If, for instance, he has intercourse with his wife or some other woman, it may happen that the *wakáni*, who is con-

---

[5] Every death that takes place within the family of the slayer during the time following the killing of the enemy is set down to the secret operation of the revengeful spirit (*wakáni*). At a feast where I was present the slayer told me that within his family seven persons had died of mysterious diseases or through accidents during the two years which had elapsed since he killed his enemy. This *wakáni*, therefore, was considered to have been a particularly bad one.

[6] The deer, according to the idea of the Jibaros, is the incarnation of a demon (*iguanchi*), one of the most dangerous animal demons they know. The Jibaros, therefore, never eat the flesh of the deer or even touch it with their hands.

stantly lurking near him, slays him, so that he dies on the spot. Besides, since there is supposed to exist an intimate connection between woman and the plants which she cultivates, the consequence of his having intercourse with his wife will be that the manioc and other fruits, recently planted for the feast, will not reach ripeness, but will dry away. If the slayer eats some unsuitable and forbidden food the spirit may again through this food operate against him, causing indigestion and death. On the whole, the slayer must observe the principle to live as retired and hidden a life as possible, for in this way he may more easily escape his supernatural enemy. This is also the reason why he must not take part in religious feasts, or wear body painting, eartubes, necklaces, and other magical ornaments used by those who enter into relation with the spirits, and through which these, as it were, are challenged.

Under such circumstances it is easy to understand that the Jibaro warrior conscientiously submits himself to the severe rules imposed upon him by society, and that the feast itself is prepared and celebrated with all the care which custom and tradition require.

It may be observed that the practices and rites of the feast *numbuimartinyu* and the rules observed afterwards may vary in certain details among different tribes. Thus among the Jibaros of the Pastaza and the Canelos Indians the diet of the slayer after the " washing of the blood " consists mainly of the fruit and the leaves of the plant *mandi* (called *sangu* by the Jibaros). During a whole year the slayer has to abstain from cohabiting with his wife. The lance among these Indians is not washed at the ceremonial bath in the river, but the point of it is roasted in the fire so that the blood is dried or burned.

The lance or the rifle with which an enemy has been killed is always looked upon with superstitious fear by the Indians, and is never more used in hunting. If, for instance, a wild hog is killed with such a lance or rifle, the flesh of the animal is supposed to get the same taste as human flesh, and would not therefore be eaten by anybody. The Jibaro warrior therefore is anxious to exchange as soon as possible the lance with which he has killed an enemy. The rifle he generally keeps, but no longer uses it in hunting but only in wars.

Immediately after the feast *numbuimartinyu* the slayer repairs to a natural waterfall in the forest (*paccha* or *sasa*), situated at a distance from his home, and takes some baths to further purify himself. He remains here alone for three days, fasting and taking tobacco water, sleeping at night in a small ranch and paying particular attention to his dreams. After the lapse of the three days he returns to his home, but passes the first two nights not in his

house but in a small ranch made at the bank of the river. Thereafter he can sleep in his house, not with his wife, however, but in
the fore room or men's department of the house.

SUAMARTINYU, "THE FEAST OF PAINTING WITH GENIPA (SUA)."

The feast *suamartinyu*, which is held three or four months after
the *numbuimartinyu*, takes its name from the main ceremony performed, the painting of the slayer with genipa (*sua*). Even at the
numbuimartinyu, as we have seen, painting with *sua* took place, but
that procedure is now undertaken more thoroughly and assumes a
greater importance than at the feast first mentioned.

A detailed description of the feast *suamartinyu* is not necessary,
since the ceremonies which take place are exactly the same as those
performed at the final great *tsantsa* feast. The *suamartinyu*, as a
matter of fact, is only an anticipation of the latter. The only difference is that the preparations for the feast *suamartinyu* are less
grand, fewer swine and chickens are slaughtered, and fewer guests
are invited. The principal ceremony at this feast is the washing of
the trophy in a magical solution, through which the spirit of the
slain enemy is supposed to become the slave and will-less instrument
of the victor. Then follows the ceremonial slaughtering of the
swine, and the final ceremony when the *whuéa* or priest helps the
slayer to dress himself, cuts his hair, makes him break the fast, and
lastly paints his face, breast, stomach, arms, and legs with *sua*. The
feast *suamartinyu* lasts three or four days.

At the painting of the slayer's body with genipa the Jibaros formerly used a special instrument consisting of a cylindrical object,
made of a special kind of very hard clay, into which certain circle-
formed ornaments were incised. The instrument was dipped into
the genipa solution and rolled along the cheeks, arms, legs, etc., of
the slayer, the ornaments incised in the instrument being thereby
stamped upon his body. This instrument, which is called *payánga*,
is still known, but it is no longer made of clay, but of a kind of wood.

The object of the feast *suamartinyu* is partly to give the slayer
renewed protection against the spirit of the killed enemy, partly to
favorably prepare the trophy for what is its proper aim, namely, to
promote the material wealth of the slayer, especially for the
period immediately following the feast *numbuimartinyu*. In the
first respect the feast is of significance for him in so far that
he need no longer observe the same anxious caution and strict abstinence in his mode of life that was his obligation formerly. Thus he
may again dress completely, tie his hair in pigtails, wear face paint-

ing and ornaments, manage lances and other weapons, go hunting and fishing, take part in feasts, sleep with his wife, etc. In one word, he can in the main return to his former normal life with the exception that he is obliged to continue keeping diet. Even in this respect he has, however, far more liberty than before. With regard to food he has to observe the following rules: The slayer must absolutely abstain from eating pork and chicken. He is allowed to eat all fruits cultivated by the Jibaros, the manioc, however, only boiled, but not roasted. He must not eat the flesh of the tapir (*pamá*), of the great wild hog (*unta pakki*), of the paca (*Cœlogenys paca*, called *kashai* by the Jibaros), or of any kind of monkey. Of birds he must not eat the toucan, the wild turkey, the paugi, or other larger birds commonly hunted by the Jibaros, but only such small forest birds as are shot by blowpipe and nonpoisoned arrows. On the other hand, he is recommended to eat the small peccary (*yankipi*) and the rodent guatusa or agouti (*Dasyprocta aguti*). Of fish he is recommended to eat the large *nápi* (Spanish, *bagre*), and the *wámbi* (Spanish, *bocachupa*), but is forbidden to eat the *kanga* (Spanish, *bocachico*), the commonest fish in the South American rivers. He may also eat small fish or sardines (*chumakai*). If he infringes these rules he runs the risk of falling ill and dying, and the object of the whole feast will fail.

The dietetic prescriptions just mentioned depend on the following ideas: The slayer must, as a general rule, avoid eating the flesh of any animal through which the spirit of the slain enemy may get an opportunity to harm him. The most important mission of the *tsantsa* after the feast *suamartinyu* is to promote the increase of the principal domestic animals, the swine and the chicken (*kúchi, atáshi pambártinyu*), and more particularly for the final great feast. From the very reason that the power of the *tsantsa* is in a mysterious way effective in the domestic animals mentioned, it is considered dangerous for the slayer to eat swine's flesh and chicken during this critical period, for that power may then prove destructive to him. The prohibition especially refers to swine's flesh. If the slayer eats of it, he may fall ill and die, and that is then the work of the *wakáni*. This superstition is seemingly supported by the fact that the flesh, and especially the fat, of the swine in the tropical regions easily causes affections of the liver and other disturbances of the digestive processes. With the Indians such diseases often end fatally. The danger of an uncautious diet in this respect must of course be greater for a man who during many months has observed that strict abstinence with regard to food which has been described above.

The tapir is an animal which the Jibaros in general look upon with superstition and the flesh of which they therefore rarely eat.

Formerly they have had almost the same aversion against this animal as they still have against the deer, of which they believe that it is an incarnation of a demon (*iguánchi*), a belief still held even of the tapir by the Jibaros of the Pastaza. The flesh of the wild hog is taboo to the slayer on account of the great similarity of that animal to the domestic swine, the flesh of which is strictly forbidden to him. The paca (*kashai*), although normally eaten by the Jibaros, is looked upon as a demoniacal animal, its flesh being therefore forbidden to persons who from one reason or another are obliged to diet.

That monkeys' flesh is forbidden to the slayer is due to the great likeness of these animals to man. The spirit of the dead enemy may hide in such an animal and cause the death of the slayer in case he tries to shoot it in the forest or eat of its flesh.

Similarly the soul of the enemy may temporarily take its abode in a toucan, a paugi, or some other large bird of the forest, and in this shape threaten the life of the slayer. Their flesh is therefore equally taboo to him.

The prescription that the slayer can eat the manioc only boiled but not roasted is due to the fact that at the great feast the Jibaros prepare from roasted manioc a sort of manioc wine (*shiki*), a magical drink which is ceremonially drunk on the last day of the feast. Since the consuming of this drink forms an important part of the conjurations at the feast, it is considered fraught with danger for the slayer to prematurely come in contact even with the roasted manioc of which it is made.

On the other hand, the prescriptions in regard to the diet of the Jibaro warrior are founded on the idea that by eating the flesh of certain other animals he will acquire qualities characteristic of these animals, which make it easier for him to escape his invisible supernatural enemy as well as his living relatives. From this point of view we have to explain, for instance, the recommendation for the slayer to eat the flesh of the agouti. This small rodent is very shy and runs fast, being rather difficult to catch. By eating the animal the slayer will acquire the same quality, at present very useful to him. Similarly the fish *wámbi* is known as very shy and quick, great skill being required for catching it. The large fish *nápi* also cunningly hides in the depths of the great rivers and lagoons, thus easily escaping his persecutors. Even this fish, therefore, possesses qualities which are useful for the Jibaro warrior who is trying to evade his enemies.

The prohibition for the slayer to eat the fish *kanga* is explained from the mythological ideas of the Jibaros. According to these, as already mentioned, all animal beings, even the fishes, have once been men—that is, Jibaros. Even in primitive times they used to wage war on and kill each other, to make trophies of each others' heads and to celebrate *tsantsa* feasts. The fish *kanga*, then, in a fight had been killed by one of his enemies, who later on was changed into a bird, the umbrella bird, called *ungúmi* by the Jibaros. The *ungúmi* also made a trophy of the head of the fish *kanga*. Therefore the mouth of the *kanga* has still great similarity to the reduced mouth of a human *tsantsa*, and this is the reason why the Jibaro warrior, during the time he has to fast, abstains from eating that fish.

The object of the feast *suamartinyu*, on the other hand, was said to be to promote the material wealth of the slayer, especially for the period falling between this feast and the final victory feast. For the latter he has to make very large preparations and, so to speak, start his economic life from the beginning. Apart from some smaller preparatory work, he has first of all to breed a number of swine and chickens to be slaughtered at the feast, and to make new plantations of manioc, plantain, and other fruits, which will be eaten by the guests. All these preparations, and especially the breeding of the swine which must become full grown, require about two years. Now, according to the idea of the Jibaros, it is precisely the *tsantsa* which will cause the domestic animals and the fields to grow and develop not only in a normal way, but with an extraordinary force. The Jibaros do not find anything contradictory in the thought that the spirit of the slain enemy on the one hand entertains feelings of hatred and revenge against his slayer and always looks for an opportunity to harm him, and on the other hand, at the same time, as it were, plays a rôle as his friend and adviser. The latter, it must be understood, he has become under the influence of the magical conjuration, through the ceremonies performed at the feast *suamartinyu*. It is therefore of paramount importance that these ceremonies should be carried out in the proper way and with due care, just as it is important that the slayer himself should continue strictly to observe the rules of fasting.

After the feast *suamartinyu* the slayer undertakes a small journey, just as he did after he had "washed off the blood." Before he can make use of the greater liberty with regard to his mode of life which is conceded to him after the said feast, it is considered necessary that the black painting applied to his body at the feast should have completely disappeared. The black dye prepared of the fruit of the *Genipa americana*, owing to its richness in tannin, is very astringent, and in spite of any washing does not leave in less than four or five days. The slayer as usual retires to the forest, staying in the neighborhood of a *sasa*, where he bathes repeatedly, and sleeping at night in a small ranch made close by. After the lapse of some days, when there are no traces left on his body of

the painting, he returns to his home, where he, in the main, resumes
his former normal life, the only exception being the fasting which
he is still bound to observe.

During the time following the slayer continually has intercourse
with the spirit of the enemy he has killed, whom he meets and con-
verses with, especially in his dreams. Through the ceremonies of
conjuration performed, the *wakáni* is now turned into his obedient
slave, and is obliged to put his superhuman power and knowledge at
his disposal. The spirit gives his victor instructions and advises him
as to how the swine and the chickens ought to be fed and taken care
of in order that they may grow quickly, get fat and increase, or how
the plantations ought to be attended to, cleaned and irrigated in
order that they may flourish and bear abundant fruits. In the dream
the spirit shows to the slayer the tracks of the numerous swine which
will be the result of such care, and he lets him hear the sound of
their grunting. The latter also believes that he sees his house surrounded by large flourishing plantations of manioc, bananas, sweet
potatoes, and other fruits, even they being the future result of the supernatural power of the *tsantsa*. The fact that the slayer, through his
intercourse with the *wakáni*, becomes invested with an extraordinary
insight in all domestic works, also explains why during this time he
becomes the adviser of the women at the attendance of the domestic
animals and at the cultivation of the fields, occupations that normally,
according to the division of labor prevailing among the Jibaros, are
incumbent solely upon the women. With the *tsantsa* hanging round
his neck he now and then goes out in the swine yard and gives the
women instructions with regard to details of attendance of the animals, or out to the manioc plantations where he gives them similar
prescriptions concerning agriculture.

During all this, however, great caution and care is still necessary
for the victor. If he, for instance, is negligent in observing the rules
in regard to fasting, it may happen that the result of the whole thing
turns out contrary to the one expected. Through such negligence he
not only exposes himself personally to danger, but it may also happen
that the swine, instead of growing and increasing in number, will die,
through the *wakáni*, in the shape of a poisonous snake, biting them to
death, or killing them in some other way. The plantations likewise,
instead of flourishing and giving fruits, may dry away. All these
calamities are operations of the revengeful spirit, against whom sufficient precautions have not been taken.

In case, however, everything has turned out well, if the swine have
become full grown and fat, if the fields have given abundant fruits
so that there is a good supply of manioc, bananas, and sweet potatoes,
the warrior begins to take steps for the celebration of the proper
victory feast, the so-called *einsupani*.

THE TSANTSA FEAST—EINSUPANI

The general name for a feast among the Jibaros is *nambéra,* which word, however, particularly signifies a drinking feast. The *tsantsa* feast is, therefore, sometimes called *nambéra tsantsa.*[6] The technical name for this feast is *einsupani,* from *ein(t)su,* "folk," "people," and the word "*pani,*" which also seems to mean "feast," but is only used in this and a couple of other words.[7] "To celebrate a feast" means *ihiámbrama,* whereas the verbal substantive *ihiámbratinyu* signifies the person who makes the feast, or in whose honor it is held. The principal person at the *tsantsa* feast—that is, the slayer—is also entitled *mangértoma* ("the one who has killed"). As a host at the feast he is called *heindinyu.*

The *tsantsa* feast is also sometimes called *tsantsa yuoma*—that is, "the eating of the *tsantsa*"—which expression especially has reference to the series of conjurations through which the spirit of the killed enemy is trodden under foot, mortified, and enslaved. When the Jibaro is speaking of an enemy whom he particularly hates and wants to kill he says of him: "*Yuotahei*"—"I will eat him." This expression may be a survival from a time when the Jibaros were cannibals, and as a matter of fact at the head feast, as we shall see, a ceremony has formerly taken place which may be regarded as cannibalism.

The final *tsantsa* feast generally takes place about one and a half or two, sometimes even three or more, years after the *suamartinyu,* according to the thoroughness with which the victor wants to prepare himself for the same. One or two months before the preparations proper begin the slayer returns to that life of a penitent which was prescribed for him during the period between *numbuimartinyu* and *suamartinyu.* He thus is not allowed to wear other clothes than his loin cloth, keeps his hair untied, resigns all ornaments and facial painting, does not bear a lance, does not go out hunting or fishing, abstains from sleeping with his wife, etc. His diet also is much the same as then. From now until the feast is over he eats only fruits, manioc, bananas, sweet potatoes, etc., but only boiled, not roasted.

All preparations for the feast are made by the slayer himself, who also acts as host at the feast. In this quality he has to attend to several representative duties.

One and a half or two months before the feast the women commence to make the many clay vessels needed, a work which they continue for some weeks. Among these clay vessels there are large

---

[6] The word *hista,* which is now most frequently used for a feast (*tsantsa hista,* etc.), is borrowed from Spanish (*fiesta*).

[7] *Kusúpani,* "the feast of the men," and *Yaurápani,* "the feast of the dogs."

pots (*muitsa*), in which the great quantity of manioc beer brewed for the feast is kept, and smaller dishes (*pininga*), used for the food and the drink. The large pots are painted red with ochre, but without ornaments. Some of them, however, have triangular black figures painted at the mouth. Even the *piningas* have the outside uniformly painted red with ochre; the inside, on the other hand, is adorned with various ornamental figures on a black ground. The black paint used is a sort of wax, called *sekáta*, produced by certain wild bees, which is melted at the fire for the purpose of painting. The ornaments represent spirits (*wakáni, yusa*), often with the arms stretched out, and snakes, especially the great boa serpent (*pangi*), and some of the most poisonous snakes known to the Indians, as well as butterflies (*wambishku*). Triangles and other linear ornaments are also common. The Jibaros on the Rio Pastaza usually paint the outside of the *piningas* with white ornaments on a red ground.

Some *piningas* are made quite small, about a third or a fourth of the normal size. These are intended for certain persons, who at the feast take part in important conjurations, and hence have to fast afterwards, being allowed to drink only a small quantity of manioc beer.

A quite small pot is made with special care. In this pot, managed by the priest or *whuéa*, the juice of tobacco is kept, which is given to the slayer and some other persons at the feast before and during certain important ceremonies. The pot is called *nattipya*, and is provided with a small cover, from which the women taking part in the ceremonies have to drink the juice of tobacco. The pot and the cover are likewise painted red with ochre.

More multifarious are the preparatory works incumbent on the men. At first they make a number of benches of split bamboo (*guadúa*) of almost square form, each side about 1½ meters in length, which are placed along the walls of the house and also in the middle close to the central pillars of the fore room (*tangámasha*). These benches, which are called *peáka*, serve as seats during the day and as bedsteads during the night. For feasts some new ones must always be made for the guests who pass the nights in the house. Some small round seats (*kutánga*), for one man to sit upon, are also made. One of these is made with special care. Upon this *kutánga* the principal person of the feast, the slayer, will sit during the ceremonies.

The fetching of a number of large chonta trunks from the forest also belongs to the earlier preparations for the feast. They will serve as firewood at the feast, and have to be brought in good time in order that they may dry.

Two or three weeks before the feast the younger men are sent to hunt in the forest and to fish in the small rivers. These hunting and fishing expeditions before a feast are considered very important, for a good supply of game and fish must be procured for the guests. Generally these expeditions last for 15 days. The game and fish are always brought home in a dried condition.

The fishing is carried out by varvasco poison (*Jacquinia armillaris*), called *timo* by the Jibaros. With this poison the water is poisoned in a certain part of the small river chosen for the purpose, the river being previously barred with sticks and stones.

Two weeks before the feast some heads of green bananas are hung up on the ceiling of the house, in order that they may get yellow and ripen. Ripe bananas (*tsamá*) form one of the dishes offered to the guests at the feast.

The last work which has to be performed by the men consists in weaving a dozen large baskets (*changina*), used by the women at the feast for carrying home the great quantity of manioc, camote, and other fruits needed for the daily common banquet. The work is done by the younger male members of the family, as well as by their friends from other houses. The slayer himself goes around to the houses inviting the younger men, his most intimate friends, to help at the work. The youths at first go out into the forest in order to collect the liana used for basket weaving, called *câpi*, and thereafter assemble in the house of the feast giver, where the work takes place. It lasts for two or three days. When it is finished the slayer expresses his thanks to the young men for their help, addressing each of them separately with a few words and at the same time inviting them to the feast.

During these days the victor has been engaged in inviting other people also to the feast, going around alone from house to house. The invitation is always made in a ceremonial way, the slayer addressing the person concerned in a sort of speech and speaking in a loud voice. While thus wandering about in the houses, the slayer does not carry his lance, but only a staff, in observance of the rules prescribed for him with regard to the wearing of arms.

A few days previous to the arrival of other guests, two old persons arrive in the house who will play important rôles at the feast. One is an old man and warrior, who himself has killed some enemies and celebrated at least one *tsantsa* feast. This man is called *whuéa*, and may be said to act as priest at the feast, all ceremonies being carried out with his assistance. In most cases he is the same person who conducted the ceremonies at the feasts *numbuimartinyu* and *suamartinyu*.

The other person is an old woman, called *oháha*, who at the feast will conduct all ceremonies performed by the women, especially the incantations and conjurations, acting thus, as it were, as a priestess. She has also led such ceremonies at the earlier minor feasts. Both the *whuéa* and the *ohába* are paid for their services, the former receiving from the slayer an *itipi* (loin cloth), the latter a woman's garment (called *tarachi*). They also receive some flesh from the swine slaughtered at the feast.

The Dance "Wuimenshi"

Immediately after the basket work is finished, a dance, or rather a series of conjurations, takes place, which, on account of the word *wuimina* (" go away ! ") often pronounced therein, is called " *wuimenshi.*" This dance, which may be regarded as an introduction to the feast proper, is performed during the four last nights before the latter commences, and its aim seems to be in part to paralyze the danger which is supposed to proceed from the *tsantsa*, in part to increase the magical power of the trophy and make it effective in different departments of the economic and social life of the Indians. With the dance *wuimenshi*, therefore, the *tsantsa* feast may be said to begin.

This dance and the corresponding conjurations are performed by the younger men and women, especially by the men, the nearest friends of the slayer. In the first place those youths take part in it who made the baskets. The rest of the guests do not arrive until some days later, when the feast properly begins.

As is the case with most Indian dances, the *wuimenshi* commences when darkness sets in, about 6 o'clock. The slayer himself, in his quality of host, goes around the house and invites his friends to take part in the dance.

The men do not dress in festival dresses for this dance; the women again, as usual, wear the rattles of snail shells around the waist.

Wuimenshi is a ring dance. All men and women arrange themselves in a circle round the central pillar of the house and move round in slow time, holding each other's hands.

The dance is accompanied by conjurations. The first conjuration especially refers to the game; the dancers enumerating all those quadrupeds and birds which are most hunted by the Jibaros. First of all, different kinds of monkeys are mentioned, which are much appreciated by the Indians on account of their flesh, their fur, and their teeth. The *tsantsa* thus, by virtue of its supernatural power, among other things will promote the hunting luck of the victor. From the last incantations it moreover appears that it will also exert a favorable influence upon the home industry of the Indians— weaving, basket raddling, etc.

The *wuimenshi* is begun with shrill whistles. Thereafter the dancers proceed to enunciate the respective words, moving round the pillar, each word being followed by a sonorous "*hej!*"

The conjuration runs as follows:

Hej, hej, hej!

Yákuma, hej! (*yákuma*=the howling monkey, *Myletes*).

Kapándinyu, hej! (*kapándinyu*=the red one; the howling monkey is of red color).

Chua, hej! (*chuo*=the brown monkey).

Washia, hej! (*washi*=the black monkey, *Ateles niger*).

Sepura, hej! (*sepura*=a smaller, black, long-haired monkey).

Tsiria, hej! (*tsiri*=the capuchin monkey, *Cebus*).

Tsema, hej! (*tséma*=a small gray monkey).

Pákkia, hej! (*pakki*=the wild hog).

Kávashua, hej! (*kavashu*=the green parrot).

Púsurshua, hej! (*púsurshu*="the long-tailed one").

Máshua, hej! (*máshu*=paugi, *Crax paugi*).

Kuchia, hej! (*kuchi*=the domestic pig).

Kúturama, hej! (*kúturama*="the fat one").

Áyandasta, hej! (*áyandasta*=the women's clothing).

Ikichia, hej! (*ikichi*=girdle to confine the clothing with).

Changina, hej! (*changina*=raddled basket), etc.

This conjuration is continued for about one hour, the dancers meantime moving alternately to right and to left. Every time they stop to move in the opposite direction they give loud whistles and shouts of "*chi, chi, chi, chi,*" as if to keep up with these shouts the continuity of the conjuration.

Another conjuration is devoted to women and the fecundity of the women. The fruitfulness of the women, therefore, will be one more of the beneficial effects of the *tsantsa*.

This conjuration is as follows:

Hej! hej! hej!

Noa, hej!

Noa, hej!

Kanutpia, hej!

Kanutpia, hej!

Nihantsi suruchu kanutpia, hej!

Kanutpani hitia, hej!

Numbintinya, hej!

Nihīrseisaka, kahetpia, hej!

Noa, hej!

Noa hej!

Kahetpia, hej!

Nikasneiti, hej!

Eitgamue, hej!
Pingerati, hej!
Maketi, hej!

The word *noa* means " woman." *Kanutpia, kahetpia, numbintinya, nihĩrseisaka*, are different expressions for the sexual act. *Nihántsi surúchu*=" may the *tsantsa* grant it;" *"nikasneiti"*=" may it be true;" *eitgamue*=" so we will do;" *pingerati*=" may it be nice;" *maketi*=" it is enough."

Of an altogether different kind is the conjuration now beginning. It is the mysterious song to the bird *kungúpi*, a word therein repeatedly pronounced. The soft melody seems to indicate that the song of *kungúpi* is in part a prayer, in part a conjuration. The youths, while singing, dance in a ring round the pillar as before.

The melody is the following:

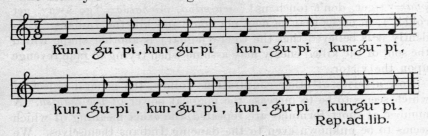

Kungúpi is a mysterious nightbird which the Jibaros regard with superstitious dread, believing that the soul of the murdered enemy may take the shape of that bird and then send them sickness and death. Whether we are here dealing with a purely mythical bird, or a really existing one, I have not been able to ascertain. To the mind of the Jibaros, of course, it is a real bird; but no one of the whites living in the regions inhabited by these Indians knows anything about the bird *kungúpi*. Very long ago, the Jibaros told me, one of their ancestors had suddenly died at a feast, and his death was ascribed to the bird *kungúpi*, the shape of which the killed enemy was supposed to have taken. Since that time, at every *tsantsa* feast, they sing a special conjuration to the ominous bird in order to prevent the repetition of such an incident.

Having for a while merely repeated the word *kungúpi* in a certain melody, the dancers continue with the phrases *mana, michaki, kungupi, kungupi*, and *wuimina, michaki, kungupi, kungupi*, which is a formula for conjuring away the fatal bird (*wuimina*=go away; *michaki*=" may you get cold!" " may you stiffen!"—an expression frequently used in similar conjurations).

Another conjuration of the same kind is the following chant:

Yawanu ikyama,
Yawanu ikyama,

Yawartaki takarseipya,
Wuimina chianga,
Huimya, huimya,
Wuimina chianga,
Wuimina chianga,
Umaná michakia,
Wuimina michaki,
Umaná chiangá,
Umaná chiasua,
Umaná chiángá,
Núruna chásamana,
Tahitá chiangana, etc.

In this chant it is particularly "the tiger in the forest" (*yawanu ikyama*) that is the object of the conjuration (*yawartaki takarsei-pya*="tiger, don't touch us!" *wuimina, michakia*="go away, get cold!"), in order that he may not come and kill the Indians. Evidently it is believed that the tiger (jaguar) is another shape which the soul of the killed enemy may assume when trying to take revenge upon the victor.

Now a series of other conjurations follow, the general object of which seems to be to increase the magical power of the *tsantsa*. A number of short formulas are repeated, the exact meaning of which seems to be unknown even to the dancing Indians themselves. We are here dealing with an archaic or ceremonial language which, at the most, is understood by some of the oldest Indians. The dancing youths repeat the same phrase for about an hour. Then some old Indian recites another similar formula of conjuration in a special melody, and this is in its turn repeated for a while in the same way. Each formula is finished with shrill whistles and shouts of "*chi, chi, chi,*" and such exclamations also accompany the interruption which takes place when the dancers change from the right to the left and vice versa. Examples of such formulas, unintelligible as to their exact meaning, are the following:

Mainia mainiatekana.
Kukuyukunta kunyukunta.
Sivu, sivu, sivahamba.
Sirumbachi wahe, etc.

The dancers thus, for instance, during half an hour may incessantly repeat the formula *mainia mainiatekana, mainia mainiate-kana,* continuing thereafter with another formula.

Other formulas of conjuration are more intelligible, as for instance the following:

(A)mue sinchimaka, chikichitantani, aya, aya,
(A)mue sinchimaka, himeritantani, aya, aya:

"Make thee strong, make thee powerful, my only tsantsa."

In the ceremonial language the Jibaros often make use of certain Quichua words, which are very rare in their language. The word *sinchi* is Quichua and means "strong"; and likewise the word *aya*, which means "soul," "dead man." In the formula mentioned the soul of the enemy, materialized in the *tsantsa*, is directly spoken to.

The phrases are in most cases recited quite monotonously or nearly as when one speaks. In other cases they are sung in a special melody, as in the following chant directed to the *maikoa*, the most important narcotic drink of the Jibaros:

"*Maikoa make sinchi; maikoa make sinchi.*"

"Make the *maikoa* strong; make the *maikoa* very strong."

During the days that the dance *wuimenshi* takes place the *tsantsa*, enveloped in a cloth, is kept hanging over one of the fires in the house in such a way that it is continually touched by the smoke from the fire. The object of keeping the trophy in this way is partly to kill the microbes which are likely to destroy it, partly, as it seems, to mortify the spirit of the dead enemy. The spirit (*wakáni*), according to the idea of the Indians, always keeps in the neighborhood of the *tsantsa* and now and then approaches the head in the ghostly, invisible shape of a man. During the dance and the conjurations the Indians at times move away from the chonta pillar round which they dance and make a tour of the house, when they also approach the trophy hanging over the fire and chant to it.

The slayer himself does not take part in the dance, but he is not allowed to sleep at all during the night. Sitting on a sort of chair of honor specially made for him, he merely looks on at the performance, only now and then giving the young men a sign to stop dancing or to begin again. Outside the ring some old women take their stand, offering manioc beer to the dancing men and women, who by turns step out from the ring to empty a *pininga* of the drink. As a rule, the women only take part in the beginning of the dance; the men, on the contrary, have to continue with it until dawn. At 6 o'clock an older Indian comes and gives three strokes with a staff to the chonta pillar round which the dancers move. This is a signal for them to finish the dance for that night. All the young men and women now run out and down to the river, where they bathe. All the dances of the Jibaros are finished with such a general bath in the river.

The dance *wuimenshi* is also continued during the following three nights.

THE PREPARATION OF THE MANIOC BEER (NIHAMÁNCHI) AND THE MANIOC WINE (SANGÚCHA SHIKI)

The following day, that is, three days before the feast proper begins, the manioc beer to be served to the many guests, and also a manioc wine which is to be drunk at the end of the feast, are prepared. The preparation of both these drinks, and especially of the manioc wine, is of a ceremonial character. The main thing is to make them as strong as possible, this being essential for the success of the feast. The slayer himself, therefore, must personally assist in the work, in order to transfer his own power to the beverages. The leading principle in the whole *tsantsa* feast, as already mentioned, is that the slayer, by virtue of the close relation established between him and the spirit of his victim, becomes invested with supernatural power and knowledge which he is trying to use for his own ends and to make effective in different departments of his economic life.

Early in the morning all the women, headed by the wife of the slayer and the priestess (*oháha*), go out to the manioc fields to fetch the manioc for preparing the drinks mentioned. Each of the women carries one of the baskets (*changina*) just made, and they are accompanied by the men armed with lances. The manioc which is to be brought home by the wife of the slayer, and of which the important manioc wine is to be prepared, is gathered with especial care. When the woman pulls up the first stalk of manioc—which ought to be particularly large and well grown—the priestess is holding her wrist and likewise helps her to lay it down in the basket. She then fills the basket with other manioc fruits without the aid of the priestess. The women return to the house with their baskets in about two hours, and at once start the preparations. The fruit is washed and the majority of it is peeled, parted, and boiled in various large clay pots. From this manioc, through masticating and mashing the fruit, fermented manioc substance is later prepared.

The manioc wine (*shiki*) is prepared in another way. For this purpose the manioc is first roasted, not boiled, a work performed by the priest (*whuéa*) at a big fire outside the house (pl. 5, *b*), with the assistance of some other Indians. As soon as a sufficient quantity

of the fruit has been roasted it is taken into the house and laid on
some large banana leaves. At the side of it three baskets (*changina*)
are placed, which are to be filled with the roasted fruit. A heap
of certain large forest leaves, called *kachīni* by the Jibaros, and another heap of a smaller kind of leaf called *wambá*, are also placed
close by. On a special banana leaf there is a piece of salt and a
piece of the stem of the manioc plant with the rind, which has previously been roasted.

Now, the roasted fruit has to be laid in the three baskets, and at
this the slayer himself and his wife and daughter have to assist,
the priest (*whuéa*) conducting the ceremonies. The latter, who has
previously prepared some juice of tobacco in his *nattipya*, gives some
of this medicine, first to the slayer and then to his wife and daughter, the first mentioned, as usual, receiving it through the nose, the
latter through the mouth. The priest subsequently grasps the slayer
by the wrist, and the latter leans down and takes one of the large
kachīni leaves and lays it carefully down upon the bottom of one of
the three baskets. Thereupon he, with the aid of the priest, takes one
of the smaller *wambá* leaves and lays it in the same way in the basket
upon the first leaf. Then the slayer, whose hand is still held by the
priest, takes one of the roasted maniocs and opens it with his fingers.
An older Indian holds out the leaf with the salt and the roasted
manioc stem, the latter having previously been scraped with a knife,
so that a small quantity of a brown powder has been obtained. The
slayer with two fingers takes a little of this powder and puts it into
the parted manioc fruit. Then he takes a piece of salt, bites off a
little of it, and puts this small piece into the fruit. He then closes
the latter with his hands and lays it carefully in the basket upon the
leaves previously laid there. Exactly the same is repeated with
another manioc. The slayer opens the fruit with his fingers, puts a
little of the brown powder as well as a small piece of salt into it,
and then lays the fruit in the basket at the side of the manioc first
placed there. Thereupon he takes a large *kachīni* leaf, as well as a
wambá leaf, and lays these in the basket upon the fruit. While all
these operations have been performed the wrist of the slayer has been
held by the priest. Now the same is repeated with the wife of the
slayer, whose right hand is held by the old man. She takes a manioc,
opens it, sprinkles some of the brown powder and a little salt into it,
again closes it, and then places it in the basket upon the leaves last
laid down there. A second manioc is in like manner put into the
basket by her. Lastly, she covers the fruit with a *kachīni* and a
wambá leaf, just as was done by the slayer. Finally, the daughter
of the slayer performs the same action, putting two maniocs into the
basket and covering them with the leaves, the girl being in the same

way assisted by the priest. In all, six manioc fruits have thus been ceremonially placed in the basket.

An older Indian now continues the work of filling the basket with roasted manioc until it is nearly full, but he does it without ceremony and is not assisted by the priest. Nor is the brown powder or the salt put into the fruit. However, the last maniocs with which the basket is filled must again be laid down by the slayer, his wife, and daughter, and with the same ceremonies as before. Each of them thus, with the assistance of the priest, again places two maniocs in the basket, sprinkling some of the brown powder and a little salt into them and covering them with the leaves. The basket having been filled, the slayer, assisted by the priest, carefully covers it with leaves and ties it over with lianas.

With exactly the same ceremonies the two other baskets are filled, the slayer, his wife, and daughter always laying down the first and the last maniocs and covering them with leaves.

At the other end of the house, in the women's quarters, a sort of shelter or broad shelf has been made of split bamboo, resting upon four poles about 1½ or 2 meters in height. Under this shelter the large clay pots in which the manioc substance is laid for fermenting are later placed upon the ground. Even the three baskets containing the roasted manioc are brought here. They are not laid on the ground but are hung up to the roof by means of a special pole fixed in the ground. The slayer himself carries the baskets here from the place where they had been filled with the fruit, the priest holding his hands. The slayer takes the pole and fixes it in the ground close to one of the four poles upon which the shelter rests. Other men complete the work, fixing the pole more steadily in the ground and tying it to the other poles. The slayer, whose hands are held by the priest, lifts up one of the three baskets and hangs it upon the pole. Thereafter, with the aid of the priest, he hangs the two other baskets upon the pole.

The baskets are left hanging here for three days until the beginning of the feast, manioc wine being then prepared from them in a way to be described later. During these days the fruit will " ripen " properly; the powder and the salt put into the manioc will impregnate the fruit and exert some mysterious influence to the effect that the wine prepared from it will turn out exceedingly strong. To the *kachīni* and *wambá* leaves, placed in the baskets, some mysterious influence is also ascribed.

While this work has been done by the slayer, his wife and daughter, and some of the men, the rest of the women, headed by the priestess, have been engaged in preparing the manioc beer (*nihamánchi*). After the fruit has been boiled it has to be masticated, a work which it takes some two hours to perform. The masticating of the manioc for the feasts is a real ceremony and is called *nauma*. Generally only the women take part in it, since the preparation of the beer is a work particularly incumbent on the women. Of the fruit, however, only a part, or at the most a half, is masticated. The rest of it is only mashed. The manioc masticated is thoroughly mixed with saliva and then spat out in a number of large clay pots (*muitsa*). In each of these some of the mashed manioc is added and the whole substance is carefully stirred.

Generally the pots are now only covered with banana leaves and the substance allowed to ferment. For the great feasts, however, an especial ferment, consisting of previously chewed and fermented manioc, is added in order that the beer may turn out stronger. A small clay vessel with this ferment is kept ready. The following operations are, in the main, carried out only by the women—first of all by the wife of the slayer, who is assisted by the priestess (*oháha*). However, even the slayer himself must assist at some actions, to transfer his power to the beverage. The wife of the slayer, whose hands are held by the priestess, carries each of the pots containing the manioc substance to the shelter before mentioned, where the fermentation will take place. Six or eight large pots are thus placed under the shelter in holes previously made in the ground for the purpose. In order that the pots may stand more steadily they are supported underneath by pieces of the genipa fruit. These pieces are placed under the pots by the slayer in a ceremonial way, his hands being meantime held by the priest. The wife of the slayer, assisted by the *oháha*, now puts a little of the manioc ferment just mentioned into each of the pots, but before the ferment is put in the slayer has each time to taste a little of it. The pots are then carefully covered with large leaves by the wife of the slayer, whose hands are held by the *oháha*, and finally tied with lianas.

Some of the large clay pots are tied on the outside with strips of bast in such a way as to form ornamental figures or patterns like those formed in basket weaving. The real significance of this arrangement is not quite clear. It is possible that its object is only to give strength to the pots so that they shall not burst at the fermentation of the manioc substance. But it is also possible that some mysterious power is ascribed to the strips as well as to the ornaments formed by them—a power which will promote the fermentation and contribute to making the beverage strong. This, at any rate, is the object of the genipa fruit placed under the pots. The genipa—from which the magical black body-paint is prepared—will communicate its power to the pots and the sacred substance contained in them, a power further increased by the fact that the slayer himself places the fruit there.

It is supposed to be of essential importance that the clay pots should be placed firmly in the ground, for then the fermentation also will take place steadily, and no disturbing influences will make themselves felt.

All these preparations have taken the main part of the day to accomplish, and are not finished until the afternoon. The fermentation, which in a way is the most important detail of the whole thing, however, still has to take place. In order to hurry or favorably influence the process of fermentation all the women sit down on the ground around the pots containing the manioc substance and, led by the priestess, sing a sort of chant or conjuration. With this ceremony, which lasts for about half an hour, the preparation of the manioc beer ends.

The fact that only the women have to brew the manioc beer—which is the rule among all Indians—is due to the same reason as make the cultivation of the manioc fields a business solely incumbent on the female sex. According to the animistic ideas of the Jibaros, all plants are animated by human spirits (wakáni), some of male sex, some of female. The manioc, like most other domestic plants, has a woman's soul. Hence—according to the principle " like is best known by like "—the women have to cultivate this plant just as, in regard to the preparation of the manioc beer, they are believed to have a special power of promoting that mysterious and, to the Indian mind, unintelligible process of nature which is called fermentation.

After the slayer has, in the way described, assisted in the preparation of the manioc beer and the manioc wine, his rôle with regard to the preparations for the feast is finished. The following days and nights he has to spend outside his own house, making on the third day, when the feast commences, his solemn entrance into the same. The first two of the three nights he thus stays outside he passes in another house a few hours away from his own; the third night, again, in a ranch made at a short distance from the house of the feast. The priest (whuéa), who always must remain in the neighborhood of the slayer and take care of him, follows him on this excursion.

All the three nights that the slayer is absent his friends in the house of the feast, and particularly the young men, perform the dance wuimenshi in the same way as on the first night, from the fall of night until the dawn.

On the afternoon of the day previous to the commencement of the feast, when the slayer has been absent for two nights, the following ceremony takes place in a ranch made a short distance from the house of the feast. Some of the older Indians take the trophy, which, as usual, is kept hanging over the fire, place it upon a shield and carry it to the ranch mentioned. In this ranch the slayer and the priest now stay, and they will also pass the following third and last night there. Outside the ranch a fire is made. A chonta staff is fixed in the ground close by the fire. The priest gives the slayer juice of tobacco through the nose, then grasps his hand and makes him hang the *tsantsa* on the top of the chonta staff. With the aid of the priest, he places three small round stones, provided for the purpose, upon the fire to be heated. When they are sufficiently hot, the slayer, whose hand is held by the priest, takes up one of them by means of a stick cleft at the end, and drops it into the head through the opening at the neck, holding the trophy with the left hand. The small stone is allowed to roll to and fro in the head for a moment; then the slayer takes it out and puts it back on the fire. The priest again gives him juice of tobacco, whereupon the same procedure is repeated with the second stone, and lastly with the third one. Every time that the slayer puts a stone into the head the priest is holding his hand, and each stone, after being used in the way described, is again put on the fire, where the stones are ultimately left. The trophy is again hung on the top of the chonta staff. The priest grasps the slayer by the wrist and makes him touch the hair of the *tsantsa* with his hand, at the same time saying, " *Kakáruma, pangi ishamakaipa* "—" Have courage; do not fear the great serpent." The trophy is subsequently taken back to the house by the other men, but the slayer and the priest remain in the ranch.

As we find, the same ceremony is repeated here as was earlier performed with the trophy previous to beginning the work of preparing it. The procedure with the small heated stones seems to be merely to mortify the soul of the enemy, attached to the head, to protect the slayer against the revengeful ghost, and favorably to prepare for the important incident which will take place on the following day—the entrance of the victor into the house of the feast.

That the object of the ceremony described is essentially to paralyze the danger threatening the slayer from the dead enemy may also be concluded from the last words addressed to him by the priest in which he is warned not to fear the " great serpent." The great boa serpent (*pangi*) is the most formidable of all demons who people the spiritual world of the Jibaros. He is the original father of witchcraft; it is from his body that the sorcerers receive the poison with which their organism is impregnated and the invisible arrow (*tunchi*), which they discharge against their victims. After death the souls of the medicine men are also believed to enter into the boa. The Jibaros, like all Indians, therefore particularly fear this monster, and when they kill a boa they think that they kill a powerful sorcerer. From the above statement it appears that the giant serpent also is one of those shapes in which the spirit of the killed enemy is believed to meet the slayer.

THE FIRST DAY OF THE FEAST: UTSANDOWAI, "THE FEAST IS OPENED"

(Pl. 7)

Those guests who have come from far arrive at the house of the feast on the eve of the day fixed for the same. They do not, however, enter the house, but pass the night in provisional ranches made outside. It is not until the following morning at 5 o'clock that the doors are opened and the guests can enter. By and by the guests who live near arrive. Before entering the house all arrange their dress, which the Jibaro Indian always does when he is about to make a visit in another house. In a sort of net bag (*shigra*), carried on the back, the men have brought with them their best clothing and ornaments, first of all a new loin cloth (*itipi*). In another smaller bag they carry a comb, a small mirror, a small round gourd containing a red dye for painting the body, called *mushpa* or *aratinyu*, as well as certain other small things. At a rivulet the Indian makes his toilet; he unties his thick hair, washes it, combs it, and ties it up again in the three usual pigtails. The band with which the big pigtail at the neck is wound around is adorned with toucan feathers and human hair. On his head he places some feather ornament, a crown made of red and yellow toucan feathers, called *tawasa*, or another ornament of yellow macaw feathers, which is tied round the head, and is called *tendéarma*. Older warriors are often seen wearing a sort of cap of monkey's skin or an ornament made of squirrels' tails (*kunambi*). The face, and especially the region around the eyes, is painted red in different ways, some Indians simply coating the face with the paint, others applying geometrical patterns to it. A new loin cloth (*itipi*) is always put on before entering the house, a girdle of human hair (*akáchu*) being used to fix it with. Some additional ornaments are put on later for the dance at night.

The women always pay less attention to their dress and wear fewer ornaments than the men. The principal garment of the women is called *taráchi*, and a new one is as a rule made for a feast. Since weaving is an industry exclusively incumbent on the men, these always make the clothes of their wives. On the crown of the head the women on festive occasions generally wear a red-painted cotton band, called *tiriangsa*. In the ear lobes they wear similar sticks (*arusa*) as do the men, but much smaller, and besides, in the lower lip a small pin of wood which is called *tukúnu*. Both the *arusa* and the *tukúnu* are mostly ornamented with incised figures.

For the dances the women also paint their faces, although not as much as the men. Around their necks the women wear a necklace of beads called *shaúka*, and the upper arms are tied around

THE VICTOR, CARRYING THE TSANTSA ON THE BREAST, MAKES HIS FIRST ENTRANCE
INTO THE HOUSE

b. Arrangements for the washing of the tsantsa

a. The arriving guest is entertained with manioc beer by the wife of the host

with cotton strings called *patáki*. For the dances they always put on a broad girdle or rattle of snail shells (*kúngu*); but these rattles are not ornaments but a means of conjuration.

When the guests enter the house they are received by the hosts—the father, brothers, or sons of the slayer—with a ceremonial greeting (pl. 8, *a*). The men generally enter three or four at a time. Each of them utters a loud: "*Winyáhei*," "I come," whereupon all arrange themselves in a row close to the door, with their lances stretched forth, and remain motionless until they are spoken to by the hosts. Some of the boys in the house step forward and hand a small round chair (*kutanga*) to each of the guests, who now take a seat, but still without uttering a word, and holding their lances between their knees. The hosts, having arranged their dress and painted their faces, take their seats, each sitting in front of the guest to whom he is going to speak, and only utter the word "*wiñīti*," "may you come." This is the signal to the guest that he may start speaking. He mentions that he has been invited to the feast, that he has accepted the invitation and arrived to honor the victor, etc. The conversation mostly turns about the feast, the preparations made for it, the number of swine bred for the same, the number of guests invited, etc. The host and the guest speak in turns, but they do not speak in an ordinary conversational tone, but shout, and the words follow so quickly upon each other that to an outsider it is almost impossible to understand what they say. Each conversation lasts for about 10 minutes, and each guest has to be spoken to separately by some one of the hosts. During the conversation manioc beer is repeatedly served to the guests by the women in the house. Each guest has to empty at least three dishes (*pininga*) of this drink. After this ceremonial reception the guests may step forth from the door and move about in the house at liberty; and other guests arriving are received in the same manner.

Only the men are received in this ceremonial way. The women, following their husbands, fathers, or brothers, enter without any form of salutation and are not particularly spoken to by the hosts.

All the guests having arrived and been properly received by the hosts, preparations are immediately made for receiving the victor himself, whose solemn entrance now takes place.

Some of the oldest warriors take the trophy, which has been kept hanging in the smoke over the fire, place it on a shield and carry it to the ranch outside of the house, where the slayer and the priest have passed the third night. Here, in part, the same ceremony is repeated as took place on the previous day. The *tsantsa* is placed on the top of a chonta stick fixed in the ground. The priest gives the slayer juice of tobacco and helps him to hang the trophy on himself, over the breast. The priest takes his stand immediately behind the slayer, and behind them the other warriors range themselves in a row, armed with lances, shields, and firearms. All proceed, slowly and ceremoniously, toward the house, the priest holding his hand upon the shoulder of the slayer. In front of the latter another old Indian goes, holding the chonta stick in his hand. He fixes the stick in the ground a few steps in advance of the slayer. As soon as the latter, walking slowly, has reached the chonta stick the old man removes it, and again fixes it in the ground some steps in front of the slayer, and so on until they reach the door of the house. During this march the slayer repeatedly receives juice of tobacco through the nose, administered by the priest. At the door the procession stops. The slayer takes off his old loin cloth and puts on a new one which is held ready. Then, with the aid of the priest, he takes off the trophy, which is tied to a chonta lance. The priest takes the lance, with the trophy tied to it, quickly passes it in through the door, takes it out again, and again passes it inside, fixing it firmly in the ground close to the door.

Meanwhile the other men and the women arrange themselves to receive the victor, whose entrance into the house takes place under the same ceremonial conditions as at the feast *numbuimartinyu*. Now, just as on that occasion, the dance *ihiámbrama* is performed, the wife and daughter of the slayer playing the principal part among the women. The women appear from the interior of the house, arranged in a row, holding each other by the hands, with rattles of snail shells around their waists. Foremost of the women are the wife and daughter of the slayer. On each side of them the men stand in two rows.

Immediately before the dance *ihiámbrama* takes place, two warriors rush into the house from outside, between the rows, brandishing lances and shields and giving war cries as if they were charging against an enemy. They are followed by a third warrior brandishing a rifle, with which he fires a shot in the air. These warriors are preparing the way for the victor. The latter now receives juice of tobacco from the priest through the nose, and his wife and daughter receive it through the mouth. The daughter then seizes the slayer from behind at the waist with both hands, while his wife, heading the rest of the women, gives him her right hand. All now dance into the interior of the house to the accompaniment of rattles, drums, and flutes, and immediately return to the door. The same maneuver is repeated twice more, but the second and third times the slayer holds the *tsantsa* in his right hand, with his arm stretched out, while proceeding with the women into the interior of the house. The dance *ihiámbrama* is thus repeated three times, just as at the previous minor feasts.

The *tsantsa* is again tied to a chonta lance and the latter is fixed in the ground at the door, the usual way of keeping the trophy when it is not needed for the ceremonies.

All the ceremonies described have one and the same object: To protect the victor against the spirit of his enemy. Within the house those conjurations will take place through which the *wakáni* is trodden under foot, mortified, and completely made the slave of his conqueror. The first entrance into the house is, therefore, believed to be particularly critical for the latter. When the victor approaches the house the spirit is believed to meet him in the invisible shape of a man trying to kill him. Juice of tobacco is repeatedly given him to increase his power of resistance against the machinations of the invisible enemy. The chonta staff fixed in the ground in front of the slayer, when he approaches the house, has for its object to prevent the *wakáni* from meeting him. The three warriors, who, previous to the dance *ihiámbrama*, rushed into the house brandishing their weapons and shooting, likewise were trying to keep off this enemy and inspire him with terror, for the lance and the shield, and still more shots from firearms, are feared even by the spirits. Lastly, the object of the whole dance *ihiámbrama*, as we have seen before, is to secure the victor's first entrance into the house.

The ceremonies at the "entrance" of the victor may vary somewhat in certain details. Thus at another *tsantsa* feast the proceedings were as follows: Some of the older warriors took the *tsantsa*, placed it on a shield, and carried it with caution to the ranch outside the house, where the slayer and the priest had passed the third night. The shield, with the *tsantsa*, was set down on the ground, and all warriors started to dance around it, making menacing gestures against it with their lances. Thereafter the slayer, followed by the other warriors, began slowly to move toward the house. The priest placed the shield, with the *tsantsa*, on the ground a few steps in front of the slayer. As soon as the latter had reached the shield, the priest again moved it a short distance from him on the ground, and so on until they reached the door of the house. Here the slayer exchanged his old loin cloth for a new one. The priest made him touch the *tsantsa* with his mouth and helped him to hang it around his neck. Thereupon, the dance *ihiámbrama* took place in the way described above.

With these introductory ceremonies the official part of the morning's program is finished. A general drinking bout now commences, manioc beer being brought in large *piningas* to each of the guests by the women. Food is also offered them, consisting of boiled manioc and boiled ripe bananas, as well as of meat—game and fish.

Those persons who have played some particularly important part at the ceremonies are, however, obliged to fast. This, of course, first of all applies to the slayer himself, his wife, and daughter, who, as mentioned before, have to abstain from every kind of meat and are only allowed to eat certain fruits. The priest (*whuéa*), who assists them, both now and during the following days must abstain from eating swine's flesh. His most important duty is to prepare tobacco juice, mixed with saliva, which medicine he has continually to give to the slayer, as well as to his wife and daughter. Should he touch swine's flesh, which the persons mentioned are strictly prohibited from eating, the tobacco which he gives them would become polluted and made ineffective. Likewise the priestess (*oháha*), who conducts the ceremonies of the women, is prohibited from tasting pork. Like the priest, she, during the feast, mainly eats chicken, together with manioc and other fruits. The two warriors, who, previous to the dance *ihiámbrama*, rushed into the house with lances and shields, and the third warrior, who followed them, firing a shot into the air, are also obliged to fast on that day on account of their having taken part in an important ceremony of conjuration. Thus they are allowed to drink only a small quantity of manioc beer, which is served to them in small clay dishes specifically made for the purpose.

Later in the forenoon the preparation of the manioc wine, which was begun three days ago, is continued. The roasted manioc, which was then hung up in the three baskets, filled and arranged with so much care, is now supposed to have properly ripened. The slayer, accompanied by the priest and other men, goes to the shelter where the baskets had been hung up. The slayer, with the aid of the priest, takes down the baskets one after the other and starts to open them, proceeding with the utmost care and being always assisted by the old man. The slayer and the priest both taste the fruit in each basket to convince themselves of its having acquired the necessary virtue for the preparation of the wine. The women start to masticate the roasted fruit in the same way as the boiled manioc is masticated for brewing ordinary manioc beer. A part of the fruit masticated is then separated from the rest for the purpose of preparing a special manioc substance from it by means of fermenting it. Of this substance a kind of manioc beer will be brewed, to be drunk after the most important ceremony of the feast, the washing of the *tsantsa*, two days later. Again, of the rest of the fruit masticated the proper manioc wine (*sangucha shiki*), to be consumed on the last day of the feast, is prepared in the following way:

A clay pot is placed on the ground, and the slayer and his wife and daughter, as well as the priest, take their stand in front of it. On a banana leaf a number of wooden pins have been laid, provided from the twigs of a special wild tree which the Jibaros call *shuya* and which produces a sweet black fruit similar to grapes. On another banana leaf there have been laid some leaves of another forest tree called *apaí*. The slayer, whose hand is held by the priest, takes one of the *shuya* pins and slowly and carefully places it inside the pot— about in the middle of it—in a horizontal position. His wife and daughter, whose hands are likewise held by the priest, also put one pin each in the pot beside the first one. Another man completes the work, putting without ceremony some other similar pins into the pot until such have been laid along its whole breadth, with a distance of about half an inch between each. Now the slayer, with the aid of the priest, takes an *apaí* leaf and cautiously places it across the *shuya* pins. The wife and the daughter do the same, each laying down one *apaí* leaf in the pot at the side of the first one. Several more *apaí* leaves are laid down, until the *shuya* pins are completely covered with them. Lastly, these leaves are perforated all over with a wooden pin, so that the whole thing becomes like a sieve.

The masticated manioc substance is now laid in the pot upon the leaves. The slayer and his wife and daughter again begin the work, each of them laying down, with the aid of the priest, a small quantity of the substance. The pot is wholly filled with it, and the mouth is covered at first with some *apaí* leaves and then with some large *kachīni* leaves, the whole thing being lastly carefully tied over with lianas. The slayer, with the aid of the priest, now places the pot upon the shelter mentioned before, where it is left for two days and two nights. During this time the essence in the masticated manioc substance will be distilled and drop into the lower empty part of the pot. This essence is the manioc wine.

In the afternoon, at about 4 o'clock, two swine and some chickens are slaughtered to provide food for the guests during the two following days. The proper ceremonial slaughter does not take place until the penultimate day of the feast. The flesh of the swine now killed, however, can not be cooked until midnight, or about 1 o'clock on the following morning, and will be eaten early on the following day.

When darkness sets in, or about 6 o'clock, the general feast dance begins, which is called *hantsēmáta*. All take part in it, both hosts and guests, men and women; first of all, however, the latter. The slayer himself goes around and invites the guests to take part in the dance, speaking separately to each of them. The dance is conducted by an elderly Indian who previously gives tobacco water to the women. All who are going to take part in it are dressed in the proper way. The women, as usual, wear their rattles of snail shells around the waist. Some of the men put on additional ornaments for the dance—first of all a back ornament made of the bones of the bird *tayu* (*Steatornis*), called *tayukúnchi*, which is adorned with human hair, toucan feathers, or small stuffed birds of the forest with brilliant plumes.

The face and the uncovered part of the body is carefully painted with red ochre (*Bixa orellana*), animal figures, and figures of snakes as well as geometric ornaments being the most common patterns. The older men prefer to paint themselves black in the face with genipa. Some younger men are seen painting themselves, previous to the dance, with juice of tobacco, making with their fingers certain linear ornaments upon the face and breast—ornaments which, however, are hardly visible upon the brownish skin of the Indians. The body painting with tobacco juice is supposed to be a good prophylactic against witchcraft.

The *hantsēmáta*, which literally means: "The killing of the enemy's soul (*hantsa*)," is a ring dance. The dancers hold each other by the hands and circle around the three central pillars of the house, forming a large ring, or rather an elliptical figure, and moving alternately to the right and to the left. The women at first arrange themselves for the dance, and foremost among them are the wife and daughter of the slayer. Then follow the men, and foremost among them the slayer, who thus during the dance is standing nearest to his wife and daughter. He carries the *tsantsa* hanging on his back during the whole time. Next to him the other men take their stand. At the dance the Indians move about in the same way as in the dance *ihiámbrama*, hopping side foremost, moving first the one and then the other foot in quick time. The women hold each other under the arms, hopping with both feet at once in order that their rattles may sound more loudly. Having moved round for a while to the right, the Indians change and dance to the left for a while, and vice versa. The dance is accompanied by a chant or conjuration, and this, too, is first performed by the women. This chant principally consists in an almost monotonous refrain, "*oá, oá, oá, oá*," etc., which is sung by the women in a deep and strong guttural voice, so that the whole song gives a disagreeable, almost dismal, howling effect. When the dance reaches its climax the men also chant or shout, and the dancers seem sometimes almost to reach a state of ecstasy. Each time the men, during the dance, reach one of the doors at either end of the house, they stop for a moment, hop up and down on the spot, stamping on the ground and shouting in a loud voice: "*Hysti, hysti, hysti, hysti!*" At the same time the women hop on the spot, sounding their rattles, while the drums are beaten and the flutes played. This procedure is repeated for a long time. The dancers through this action are trying to keep off the spirit of the killed enemy, who, it is believed, is trying to enter through one of the doors to kill the victor.

During the dance certain words and phrases, adapted for the occasion, are also pronounced. Thus the name of the killed enemy is again and again mentioned, as are also the names of his relatives and the name of his native place. Similarly details of the war and of the battle, the lance with which the enemy was killed, or the knife with which his head was cut off, and even the canoe in which the victors went down, etc., are repeatedly mentioned. This dance, with short intervals, is continued until dawn. The men, however, do not take part in the dance the whole time, but sometimes leave the women alone. The latter, who are headed by the priestess, and among whom the wife and daughter of the slayer are the most active, first of all have to attend to the dance. The slayer himself also dances nearly the whole time, with the *tsantsa* hanging on his back. He is not allowed to sleep during the night.

Whereas even young girls of 8 or 10 years of age take part in the general dance, the half-grown boys seem to be excluded from it. These have another task confided to them. When the older men and women arrange themselves for the dance, the boys are placed within the ring, and when the dance commences they engage in a savage wrestling match, continually throwing each other to the ground, again rising, again wrestling, etc. This wrestling is continued for about an hour in the same violent manner, but is not repeated later during the night. As to the significance of this wrestling, the Indians only gave the explanation that it is "part of the feast." The boys, as a matter of fact, had previously been instructed by an older Indian. The wrestling thus is of a ceremonial nature, and forms part of the general conjurations.

The dance *hantsēmáta* is continued without interruption until about 1 o'clock, when there is a short interval. The flesh of the swine slaughtered in the afternoon of the day before has now to be cooked. According to the ritual of the feast, as already mentioned, the flesh of the swine slaughtered at the feast can only be cooked at midnight. On several large fires, made in different parts of the house, large clay pots are placed, which are filled with the flesh cut into pieces. During the preparations for the cooking, and while the flesh is being boiled, the dance *hantsēmáta* is continued with more vigor than before, all men and women who are not tending the fires being engaged in it. Likewise some chickens are killed and their flesh is boiled. The Indian who conducts the dance is seen dancing for a while with two or three recently killed chickens tied round his waist. The dance is supposed to hurry on the cooking of the flesh, and probably also to exert a favorable influence upon the augmentation of the domestic animals in future. As soon as the flesh is sufficiently cooked the pots are taken off the fires and lifted up on the shelves to be preserved until morning. It is not until then that the flesh can be eaten.

The dance is then continued without interruption until the morning, being attended to particularly by the women. About half past 5, or a little before dawn, all the men and women have to take part in it just as in the beginning. Having moved several times around the central pillars, all rush out from the house, continuing to hold each other by the hands, and run down to the river, where they take the usual bath. With this bath the ceremonies of that night are finished.

The Second Day of the Feast: Natéma Umártinyu, "The Drinking of the Natéma"

At about 8 o'clock the principal ceremony of the second day, the drinking of the sacred drink *natéma*, takes place. This important narcotic is prepared from a vine specially cultivated by the Jibaros, the scientific name of which is *Banisteria caapi* (of the *Malpighiaceae* family). When the drink is prepared for the feast the slayer himself has to assist in order to transfer to it the supernatural power with which he is believed to be invested.

For the preparation of the *natéma* some pieces of the stem of the vine are cut off, crushed with clubs, and parted into thinner fibers, which are boiled in water for a couple of hours. The fibers are then taken out and the drink is ready. The *natéma* drink, which has the effect of producing in the drinker peculiar visions and hallucinations which are ascribed by the Indians to certain spirits, is generally mixed with some tobacco water, through which its narcotic effects are increased. At the *tsantsa* feast the second day is regularly destined for the drinking of the *natéma*, and it is prepared and drunk with certain ceremonies, which have now to be described.

Some pieces of the stem of the *natéma* plant are laid on a banana leaf on the ground. Upon another banana leaf a larger and a smaller wooden club are laid, and with these the *natéma* stems are to be crushed. There is besides a pot in which the drink will be cooked. The priest as usual gives the slayer tobacco juice through the nose. Then he grasps him by the wrist and makes him seize a club with his right hand and a *natéma* stem with his left and crush the stem, laying it upon the other tree club. The slayer divides the stem into three or four fibers and puts them down into the pot, the priest holding his hand. Another Indian without ceremony crushes some other pieces of the *natéma* stem and arranges them in a ring within the pot. The slayer, whose hand is held by the priest, now pours some water into the pot from a water bottle and places the pot on the fire, some other men attending to the pot while it boils.

At another fire close by tobacco is simultaneously being boiled, to be mixed with the *natéma*. A small clay pot is placed by the fire, and some leaves of tobacco are laid on a banana leaf at the side of it. The slayer, whose hand is held by the priest, takes a tobacco leaf and carefully puts it, first, on the edge of the pot and then into it. The wife of the slayer repeats the process with another leaf, laying it at first on the edge of the pot and then inside it. Lastly, a third leaf of tobacco is in the same way put into the pot by the daughter of the slayer. Thereupon the slayer, assisted by the priest, pours some water into the pot and places it on the fire.

On the spot where the *natéma* is cooked there is also placed a piece of the stem of the manioc plant and two narrow strips of the bark of a tree which the Jibaros call *samiki*. The slayer takes one of the strips, winds it round his index finger, and ties it into a ring of the same size as the finger. By means of one end of the strip, which after the tying of the ring has been left free, he then attaches the ring to the piece of the manioc stem. Thereupon he in the same way makes another ring of the other strip, giving it the size of his index finger, and attaches it to the manioc stem at the side of the first ring. With the aid of the priest he ultimately places the manioc stem, with the two rings attached to it, upon the tobacco pot boiling on the fire in such a way that it rests upon the edges of the pot.

The object of this ceremony is to establish a mysterious connection between the slayer, who, as we have seen, is supposed to be filled with supernatural power, the tobacco water to be mixed in the *natéma* drink, and the manioc plant which the persons drinking of the narcotic will see in the dream. The two rings formed of the rind of the *samiki* tree will in this connection serve as mediums for the transference of the power. The Jibaros ascribe magical virtues to the *samiki* tree itself, and a little of its bark is generally mixed with the *natéma* with a view to increasing the efficacy of the drink. The basten strips of the tree having been formed into rings of the same size as the slayer's finger, are believed to catch his power, and thus to transfer it to the manioc and the boiling tobacco pot. The persons partaking of the sacred drink are afterwards, in the narcotic sleep, supposed to see, among other things, the manioc fields of the slayer in a flourishing state and bearing a rich crop of fruit.

At the *tsantsa* feast the *natéma* is only boiled for about one hour, whereupon the pot is taken off the fire. Similarly the smaller pot in which tobacco has been cooked is taken away, the manioc stick with the basten rings having first been removed. The latter is fixed in the wall close to the door, where it is left until it is dry and half consumed, being then thrown away.

The slayer, whose hands are held by the priest, seizes the small tobacco pot and pours its contents into the *natéma* pot. The drink is now ready to be consumed.

In the drinking of the *natéma* at the *tsantsa* feast both men and women, even half-grown children, take part, all " who want to dream " being allowed to drink of the narcotic. Even the slayer, as well as his wife and daughter, drink *natéma*. The drinking has throughout a ceremonial character. A number of beautifully ornamented clay dishes are placed on the ground in two rows. The priest and two or three other old men fill them with *natéma* and give them over to the persons who are going to drink. Before they give the dish to a man or woman they each time sing a long conjuration over it, summoning the *natéma* spirits. The person who receives the dish quickly empties its contents, which amount to a little more than half a liter. Immediately thereafter he or she goes out and throws up the quantity drunk (for the *natéma* at first has the effect of an emetic). Then the person again enters the house, again empties a *pininga* of *natéma*, which is given him by an old man with the same ceremony as before, and immediately again throws it up. The same process is repeated a third time. Each person who drinks *natéma* at the *tsantsa* feast thus has to empty three dishes of the sacred drink.

The persons who drink *natéma* have not previously eaten or drunk anything, and afterwards also they have to fast strictly until they have slept and dreamed. The majority of those who have drunk the narcotic leave the house and go out to sleep in some ranches of palm leaves made in the forest at a short distance from the house. Most of these are men, but at least one of them ought to be a woman, a female relative of the slayer. The slayer and his wife and daughter, who also have drunk *natéma*, do not leave the house, but have their dreams inside. The dreamers remain in the forest sleeping until the afternoon. Then they take a bath in the river and return to the house, where they tell the older Indians what kind of dreams and visions they have had. Now they are also allowed to break their fast. Their food consists only of a dish of boiled and mashed manioc and boiled ripe bananas. The dreamer has to receive the dish containing this food from the hand of the same old man who in the morning had given him or her the *natéma*.

The object of the drinking of the *natéma* at the *tsantsa* feast is to ascertain whether everything will turn out favorably for the slayer in the future, whether he will have a long life, attain to material prosperity, and be lucky in his undertakings. The slayer, as well as his nearest relatives who have drunk *natéma*, will see in the dream his house surrounded by large and flourishing plantations of manioc and bananas; they will see his domestic animals, his swine, and his chickens, numerous and fat, etc. But at the same time the persons who have drunk the sacred drink will be benefited for their own part also, being purified from impure and disease-bringing matters, and gaining strength and ability for their respective works and occupations.

The drinking of the *natéma* in the morning is as usual followed by a general drinking bout—in which, however, those persons who have drunk *natéma* do not take part—as well as by a general banquet, at which the flesh of the swine and chickens cooked during the night is eaten. With this banquet the official part of the morning's program is finished, and hosts and guests may pass the rest of the day until darkness as they like.

At about 6 o'clock in the evening the preparations for the night's dance commence, the host (i. e., the slayer) again going round in the house and inviting the guests to take part in it. All having properly dressed themselves, arranged their ornaments, and painted their faces, the *hantsēmáta* begins and is continued through the whole night exactly in the same way as on the previous night. Even the wrestling of the boys takes place for a while. The dance is continued until about half past 5 in the morning, being as usual finished off by a general bath in the river.

THE THIRD DAY OF THE FEAST: NIHANTSA NIHÁRTINYU, "THE WASHING OF THE TSANTSA"

Like all ceremonies at the *tsantsa* feast, the "washing of the *tsantsa*" commences about 8 o'clock in the morning, or about two hours after the dance of the last night has been finished. The priest (*whuéa*) has previously been engaged in preparing juice of tobacco mixed with saliva, by carefully chewing the leaves and spitting out the juice into the small clay pot (*nattipya*), from which he will apportion it out to the persons who play the principal parts in the ceremonies. A small clay pot filled with water has, by means of some strips of bast, been tied to one of the chonta pillars in the middle of the house. From this pot the priest now and then takes a little water in his mouth while chewing the tobacco leaves. The priest having in this way provided a sufficient quantity of tobacco juice in his *nattipya*, the preparations for the ceremony, "the washing of the *tsantsa*," begin.

The principal persons of the feast, the slayer, his wife and daughter, the priest, and a medicine man, assemble at a spot in the middle of the house. The women arrange themselves around them, forming a ring or semicircle, all having their rattles around their waists and

being headed by the priestess (*ohaha*).   The latter on this occasion
wears a feather ornament on her head, which normally are never
worn by the women, and also a kind of black collar prepared from
the bark of a certain tree which the Jibaros call *mupish*.   This collar, to which the Jibaros ascribe some magical power, is hung round
the neck of the priestess by the priest before the ceremony commences.

Outside the ring of the women, moreover, four warriors, armed
with lances and shields, take their stand.   The rôle which they have
to play is presently to be described.   The first thing to be done is to
provide seats for the persons mentioned—the slayer, his wife and
daughter, as well as the priest and the medicine man—and this is
done in a ceremonial way.   The wife of the slayer grasps her husband with one hand and the priest with the other hand from behind
at the waist, and all three go and fetch the seat of the slayer, which
has been placed near the wall a few steps from where the ceremony
will take place.   The slayer, both of whose hands are held by the
priest, bends down, grasps the seat, passes his hand round its edges,
lifts it up a little, immediately sets it down again, lifts it up a second
time and, accompanied by the priest, who continues holding his
hands, and by his wife, who holds both men from behind at the
waist, carries it to the spot from which they had started.   Here the
seat is ceremonially laid down on the earth, the slayer with the
aid of the priest setting it down, again lifting it up and the second
time setting it down.   Now the seat has been firmly placed, and
must not be touched by anybody until the slayer seats himself upon
it.   During these operations, both when the seat was taken up and
when it was placed upon the spot where the ceremony is to take
place, the women have been dancing around the slayer and his wife
and the priest, incessantly repeating, in slow time and almost
monotonously, the refrain: "*Chimbuyirumbá-yamáyumba, chimbuyirumbá-yamáyumba . . .*" etc., i. e., "Take up the seat,
set down the seat, . . ." etc.   Thereupon the slayer, his wife,
and the priest go and fetch another seat upon which the priest will
sit during the ceremony; and this is done in the same way as the
first time, the women dancing and singing their "*Chimbuyirumbá-
yamáyumba*" when the seat is being lifted up from the ground, and
when it is placed on the spot where the priest will sit.   The slayer's
and the priest's seats are placed opposite each other.   Three more
seats are subsequently brought for the medicine man and for the
wife and daughter of the slayer.

The slayer and the priest, accompanied by the slayer's wife, who
holds both men from behind at the waist as before, now go and
fetch a shield which had previously been placed by the door, and
which will serve as a table at the ceremony.   The shield is placed
on the ground between the seats.   At last the same persons go and

take the *tsantsa*, which as usual has been kept tied to a lance stuck into the ground at the door. The *tsantsa* is carefully placed upon the shield. On the latter are also laid the small pot containing juice of tobacco and a knife.

The slayer and the priest now prepare to sit down, each taking his stand in front of the seat intended for him. The priest lays his hands upon the shoulders of the slayer and makes him sit down on the seat, immediately raise himself, and again definitively sit down. Thereafter the slayer repeats the same with the priest, laying his hands upon his shoulders, making him quickly sit down, immediately raise himself, and again sit down. Both men now remain sitting opposite each other. Also, the three other persons take their seats, without ceremony, the slayer having the medicine man sitting on his right hand and his wife and daughter on his left.

The priest gives juice of tobacco to the slayer through the nose and to his wife and daughter through the mouth, then to the medicine man through the nose, and finally he himself also takes some. The medicine man is now the principal person acting. Taking the *tsantsa* and the knife, he takes some juice of tobacco with the point of the latter and coats the *tsantsa* with it at the neck opening. He makes a cutting motion around the neck of the head with the knife as if he were cutting it off. Then he carefully loosens the cotton string attached to the three chonta pins, which have been stuck through the lips of the head (cf. p. 31), and lastly removes the chonta pins themselves, one after the other, putting them down on the shield. Finally he gives juice of tobacco to the slayer and hangs the trophy around his neck.

While the medicine man has been engaged in these actions, the women, headed by the priestess, have been dancing around him and the other persons sitting around the shield, singing at every important moment of his operations, in the same slow, solemn time as before, the refrains: " *Chimbuyīrumba-yamáyumbá-pakéketá-kokó-kehó-shimbágasmé-mishahosé-oáoá-.* . .," etc.

Thus, when the medicine man seizes the trophy, when he makes the cutting motion around its neck with his knife, when he removes the cotton string and the chonta pins, and, lastly, when he hangs the trophy around the neck of the slayer, the women accompany all these actions by dancing, singing the refrains mentioned, and shaking their rattles. Again, the four warriors armed with lances and shields at the same time accompany the operations of the medicine man in another way: At each of the critical moments just mentioned they hold the shield, extended in a horizontal position, with the left hand, and with their lances give it from below three or four powerful resounding strokes. This ceremony is called *yaktinyu*.

The removal of the aforesaid ornaments—the cotton string and the chonta pins—has been necessary for the washing of the *tsantsa*, a ceremony which will take place outside the house. The slayer has to march out to the place destined for it, performing together with the women the same dance, *ihiámbrama*, which we know as one of the principal ceremonies from the first day of the feast. The women arrange themselves in a long column, the wife and daughter of the slayer as usual taking the foremost place. The slayer places himself at the head of them, grasping his wife with his left hand and the *tsantsa* with his right, and holding his arm stretched out. On both sides of them the men range themselves in two rows. A sign having been given, the slayer, followed by the women, proceeds dancing to the door of the house, again returns to the interior, and again proceeds dancing to the door, where he stops. He goes out, with the aid of the priest hangs the trophy around his neck, and continues a few steps toward the place chosen for the washing ceremony.

The slayer now takes a seat, placed on the ground for his use (pl. 8, *b*). On another seat his wife seats herself, and on a third his daughter. The priest and the medicine man take their stand close to them. Around these persons the women form into a ring, grasping each other by the hands. The four warriors who had performed the ceremony *yaktinyu* within the house also take up positions ready for fresh action. The priest gives juice of tobacco to the slayer and the two women, a procedure that is repeated three or four times during the following ceremonies, so that the said persons at last become narcotized, grow pale, and begin to tremble throughout their whole bodies. It is considered necessary that they should be brought to such a state, since thus they are supposed to gain power of resistance against the angry spirit during the important action which will now take place, namely, the washing of the *tsantsa*.

The medicine man fixes a chonta stick in the ground in front of the slayer. The latter takes off the *tsantsa* from his neck and with the aid of the priest places it on the top of the stick. Close to the stick a clay pot, a round gourd containing water, and a piece of the root of a liana called *sikímuro* are placed on a banana leaf. The medicine man who will conduct the washing ceremonies receives the *sikímuro* root from the wife of the slayer, who has kept it at her bosom under her *tarách*i. When the root is cut in pieces and rubbed in water it produces a white soaplike foam. It is with this soap that the *tsantsa* will be washed.

The medicine man cuts the *sikímuro* root into smaller pieces. Then the priest gives juice of tobacco to the slayer, grasps him by the wrists, and makes him pour some water into the clay pot from the water bottle. Thereupon the priest makes the slayer take up some pieces of the *sikímuro* root and put them into the pot. Now the trophy itself has to be laid down in this solution. The priest again grasps the slayer by the right hand and makes him take up a little water from the pot, with which he wets the *tsantsa*. The same operation is immediately repeated; but now the slayer also takes up a small *sikímuro* piece from the pot and touches the hair of the trophy with it. Finally the slayer cautiously puts the trophy itself down into the pot, his right hand then being held by the priest and his left hand by the medicine man.

The trophy having been laid down in the *sikímuro* solution with these ceremonies, the washing itself is performed by the medicine man (pl. 9, *a*). He rubs the hair with the *sikímuro* pieces and washes it with the soap produced by them. Having carefully soaked the trophy in the solution, he takes it up from the pot, places it on the top of the chonta stick, and continues washing it. Thereupon he begins to make it dry, shaking off the water from it, beating his arms with the hair, and drying it with his clothes. Finally he combs the *tsantsa*, receiving a special comb from the daughter of the slayer, who has kept it at her bosom in the same way as the wife of the slayer had kept the *sikímuro* root. The hair having been arranged and combed properly, the trophy is again hung on the top of the chonta stick, where it is left for a while so as to get perfectly dry. The medicine man grasps the hand of the slayer and makes him touch the hair of the *tsantsa;* then he likewise grasps the hands of his wife and daughter and makes them gently touch the trophy.

While all these operations have been performed the women, led by the priestess, have again formed a circle around the principal persons, accompanying each of the most important actions—when the *tsantsa* was first touched by the *sikímuro* solution, when it was laid in the pot, when it was washed and combed, etc.—by dancing, chanting, and shaking their rattles (pl. 9, *b*). The refrains, slowly and monotonously sung by the women, are much the same as were before sung in the house:

" *Ochoyirumbá - yamáyumbá - pakéketá - kokókehó - shimbágasmé - mishahosé-oáoá* . . . .," etc.

The operations of the medicine man have also been accompanied by the four warriors armed with shields and lances, who at the critical moments have been striking their shields performing the *yaktinyu.*

The washing of the *tsantsa* having been accomplished, the *sikímuro* solution is disposed of in the following way: The medicine man seizes the pot with both hands and pours out the majority of its contents, as well as the foam produced by the root, on the earth. The rest of the warriors start to strike the running water and foam furiously with their lances. The remainder of the solution, as well as the clay pot itself, is thrown away into the forest.

The men now make themselves ready to march back into the house. The slayer receives juice of tobacco from the priest. Then he, with the aid of the latter, takes the trophy hanging on the chonta stick and hangs it over his breast. Behind the slayer the other men, as usual, arrange themselves in a long column, all armed with their lances and guns. The priest takes his stand behind the slayer, holding his hand upon his shoulder. Some other older warriors also place themselves at the side or in front of the slayer, one of them holding the small pot containing juice of tobacco, of which a dose is repeatedly given the slayer. The women have previously returned to the house and made themselves ready to receive the slayer.

The procession now starts to move forward, the slayer walking slowly and solemnly, followed by the other warriors, continually striking the hair of the trophy with his hands. An old warrior goes in front of him, holding the comb, with which the trophy had been combed after washing, before him. The comb, by having been in contact with the victim's hair, is charged with spiritual energy, and is therefore supposed to possess the power of keeping off the spirit of the slain enemy, which according to the belief of the Indians is coming to meet the slayer when he approaches the house, trying to kill him.

The slayer stops at the door of the house. The priest helps him to take off the trophy, ties it to a lance which he quickly passes in through the door, again takes out, and passes in once more, whereupon he fixes the lance in the ground at the door inside. Within the house, meanwhile, the women have arranged themselves for the dance *ihiámbrama*, which the slayer again has to perform with the women in the way described before.

After the dance the priest takes the slayer around inside the house to manifest that he can move about in it without danger.

The object of this ceremony, the " washing of the *tsantsa*," is to " wash off " the malignity still maintained by the spirit of the slain enemy, and definitely to make it the slave and will-less instrument of the victor. This effect is first of all supposed to be brought about by the *sikímuro* solution, owing to the magical properties ascribed to the *sikímuro* root itself.

Again, the object of the dancing and chanting of the women while the washing of the trophy takes place, as well as of the ceremony *yaktinyu* performed by the four warriors, is partly to keep off the malicious spirit, who is being mortified and definitely enslaved through the washing ceremony and is more eagerly than ever trying to revenge himself, partly to give more emphasis to the ceremony itself. The refrains *ochoyirumba-yamáyumbá*, etc., belong to an

b. The women dance around the men while the tsantsa is being washed

a. The "washing of the tsantsa."

b. Dancing Jibaro man and woman

a. Jibaro man and woman in dancing dress

ancient ceremonial language, and their exact meaning is unknown
even to the Indians themselves, but their general significance is clear.
The different refrains refer to different details of the ceremonies
going on within the ring of the dancing women—when the slayer
puts the *tsantsa* on the top of the chonta stick, when he wets it with
the magical solution, when he puts it into that solution, when the
medicine man washes it, when he dries it, etc.—and they are supposed
to give more emphasis to the action taking place for the moment.
That the efficacy of an action is enhanced when it is repeated in words
is an idea deeply rooted in the minds of the Jibaros.

After the introductory dance *ihiámbrama* has taken place, and
while all are still standing in the rows in which they were arranged
for this dance, manioc beer (*nihamánchi*) has to be ceremonially
drunk. This is not a manioc beer of the common kind, but a special
beer brewed of roasted manioc (see p. 66), which is supposed to have
a particular efficacy. In front of the men, arranged in two rows, five
women take their stand, each holding a *pininga* filled with the manioc
beer. The first and the second of these women are the wife and
daughter of the slayer. The slayer himself is the first to drink of
the beer, stepping forth to the women and taking a sip from the
pininga of each of them. Then he goes back to the other men, seizes
the priest by the arm, leads him forward to the women, and makes
him in the same way drink a little from the dish of each woman,
whereupon he follows him back to the place where he was previously
standing. The same is repeated with every one of the other warriors, who have to step forward and drink by turns, according to
age and dignity, the oldest warriors who have killed many enemies
and celebrated many *tsantsa* feasts going first and the younger men
afterwards. Only the eldest men are led to the women by the slayer,
the younger men stepping forth at a sign given by him, or without
a sign, in the order in which they are arranged.

With the drinking of the *nihamánchi* the day's official ceremonies
are finished. They are followed by the usual general drinking bout
and by a common banquet. The principal persons of the feast and
other men or women who have taken part in important conjurations,
however, have to fast as before, abstaining particularly from eating
pork. The four warriors who had performed the ceremony *yaktinyu*
with their shields and lances are not allowed to drink the same quantity of manioc beer as the other men. The drink is served them, not
in the usual large *piningas*, but in the small clay dishes mentioned
before. These dishes are placed on the ground in a row and filled
with beer, and the four warriors take their stand in front of them,
ranged in a row. A sign being given them, they suddenly run forth,
all at the same time seizing their *piningas* and quickly emptying

their contents. The men thus quickly and simultaneously drinking the beer, the revengeful spirit is believed to have more difficulty in doing harm to any of them.

The drinking bout is continued nearly the whole day, until all, both men and women, get more or less drunk. In the same degree as the drink exerts its intoxicating effects, the Indians start to dance singly, and this dance goes on the whole forenoon. At first the priestess (*ohaha*) dances alone with the *tsantsa* hanging on her back, chanting a sort of conjuration. Generally, however, the younger Indians appear in couples, one man and one woman (pl. 10, *a*), the wife and daughter of the slayer being the most active among the women. The dancing couple wear the usual festival dress, the woman having her rattle of snail shells round the waist, and the man his drum, which he beats in time to the dance. The dance, generally speaking, consists in the man and the woman alternately moving to and from each other in slow, solemn time, indicated by the beats of the drum, the woman simultaneously chanting a song (pl. 10, *b*). At the same time other men accompany the dance by beating drums or playing flutes. In this way one couple after the other makes its appearance in the course of the day. Besides the priestess, other women also appear dancing alone, accompanying themselves with a chant or song. These songs generally have no reference to the feast, but the women sing whatever occurs to them in their intoxicated state. Thus it is common that at the great feasts the women address their songs to certain beautiful birds of the forest, which are then personified and spoken to. Among these birds the toucan (*tsukánga*), the cock of the rock (*sumga*), the paugi (*mashu*), and the wild turkey (*kuyu*) play the principal rôles, and the dancing women address them, giving them all sorts of pet names, praising their brilliant plumage, their walk, etc.

THE SLAUGHTER OF THE SWINE: CUCHI ACHIKTAHEI MATINYU

About 4 o'clock in the afternoon of the same day the important action takes place which the Jibaros call *Cuchi achiktahei mátinyu*—"the slaughter of the swine."

According to the ritual of the feast, the ceremonial slaughtering of the swine takes place during the night preceding the last day of the feast, or more strictly speaking shortly after midnight, "when the cocks crow for the first time," and the new day is supposed to begin. This hour is generally about 1 o'clock in the morning. Since it is, however, difficult both to slaughter a number of swine and to cook their flesh within a short time, the matter is mostly practically arranged so that the slaughtering of the animals takes place on the afternoon of the day before, whereas the cooking of the flesh is done at midnight. That the flesh should be cooked at midnight is considered absolutely necessary, for only in this case will the purpose of the whole slaughtering ceremony, the plentiful increase of the swine for the future, be attained. When the flesh of the animals killed is cooked early in the morning, at the first beginning of the new day, this will have as its consequence that henceforward there will be plenty of swine's flesh in the house of the slayer. The same holds good of the chickens which are likewise slaughtered and cooked during the first hours of the new day; but they naturally are of less importance than the swine.

As has been mentioned before, the swine to be slaughtered at a feast have been procured long before, when the first preparations for the feast began; and they are bred and fed with special care. The victor himself has supervised the rearing of these animals, giving the attending women instructions which he himself has received directly from the *wakáni*, the spirit of the killed enemy materialized in the *tsantsa*, over whom he has acquired complete domination. The number of the swine to be slaughtered at a feast is not exactly fixed in the beginning. Generally a few more are procured and bred than are supposed to be needed for the purpose. Moreover, for the propagation of the race it is necessary that at least a couple should be left alive. When the time for the great feast is approaching, the victor himself decides which of the swine are to be slaughtered and in what order it should be done. Even with regard to these details he receives advice directly from the *wakáni*, when, with the *tsantsa* hanging around his neck, he goes out into the swine yard and "points out" the animals (*kuchi aneikama*). These swine having been slaughtered in due order and their flesh consumed at the feast, the few remaining ones will increase in number all the more. This is the main idea which the Jibaros connect with the ceremonial slaughter of domestic animals at their feasts.

For a feast at which I was present 11 or 12 swine had been bred, of which 9 were slaughtered, 2 during the first day of the feast and 7 on the day of the proper ceremonial slaughter.

According to the ritual, the slaughtering should be done by some of the invited guests specially selected for this purpose. The host or his household must not touch them on any account, for then the object of the whole ceremony would be missed, inasmuch as the remaining swine would not increase. The slaughter takes place outside the house, but the animals are not all killed on the same spot, but one here and another there, close to the different walls of the house. In this way the impression is produced that the swine killed and eaten at the feast are very numerous, and the effect of this will be that they will really be numerous in future.

The animals, according to an old Jibaro custom, are killed by strangulation, without the effusion of blood. A rope twisted of lianas is tied around the neck of the swine, and a strong stick is stuck under it, the strangulation being brought about by twisting it. As the animals are thus killed they are carried into the house, where some pots with hot water stand ready. The skin is scalded with the hot water, and the hair is scraped off, whereupon the stomach is opened and the flesh cut in the ordinary way.

Of the flesh the priest and priestess receive each one thigh as a part of the payment for their services at the feast. The rest of it, with the exception of the heads and the bones, is kept on special shelves until midnight, when it is cooked. The heads and the bones, again, are roasted and kept until the day of the departure of the guests, being then divided among them.

When darkness sets in the dance *hantsēmáta*, as usual, commences and is continued, with two intervals, until dawn. The first of these intervals occurs at about 10 o'clock in evening, when the distilled manioc wine is made definitely ready. The clay pot containing the roasted and masticated manioc substance which, during the first day of the feast, had been arranged for the distillation of the drink is moved forward and placed on the ground. The priest, proceeding with the utmost care, removes the *kachīni* and *apaí* leaves with which the masticated substance had been covered. Then he removes the manioc substance itself with the same care, laying it in another vessel. Finally, in the same way, he removes the *apaí* leaves which had been laid on the *shuya* sticks collected in the pot, as well as the *shuya* sticks themselves, which together with the leaves are laid on a special large leaf. The dark-brown essence which has remained in the bottom of the pot is the manioc wine (*sangucha shiki*). The priest asks for another smaller clay pot and for a gourd, which are given him by the women. Then he pours the whole quantity of wine into the new clay vessel, and also a little into the gourd. The gourd is then placed over the mouth of the clay pot so that it covers it, and the gourd is covered with leaves; the whole thing is thereafter kept in a special place until the following morning, when the drink will be consumed.

This work being finished, the dance *hantsēmáta* is continued until about 1 o'clock in the morning, when the cocks are heard crowing, and the host declares it to be the right time to cook the flesh of the swine slaughtered. Various fires have previously been kindled in different parts of the house, large clay pots are placed upon them, and the flesh is divided up among the pots. At the same time a number of chickens are killed by wringing their necks; these are plucked and prepared on the spot, their flesh being cooked in special pots. While the cooking goes on the Indians dance the *hantsēmáta* with more vigor than usual, all the men and women taking part in it. After the flesh is boiled the pots are removed from the fires.

put aside, and kept until morning. It is not until then that the flesh cooked can be eaten, namely, at the common banquet following the last ceremony of the feast, the dressing of the victor.

The dance, as usual, is continued until dawn, when it is finished with the customary bath in the river.

The Last Day of the Feast: Nambēra Shiákma, "The Feast is Concluded"

About 8 o'clock in the morning the last great ceremony is performed with the slayer, in which the priest dresses him in a festive dress, makes him break his fast, and lastly cuts his hair and paints his body black with genipa.

The beginning of the ceremony, the carrying of the seats, the bringing of the *tsantsa* placed on a shield, etc., is exactly the same as on the previous day when the trophy was to be washed. The slayer and the priest, accompanied by the former's wife, have especially to fetch each seat upon which these persons will sit during the ceremony, a special seat being likewise brought for the medicine man. The priest helps the slayer to seat himself, and the slayer in his turn helps the priest. Between the seats the shield with the *tsantsa* has been placed. Upon the shield, besides, all those articles of clothing and ornaments are laid with which the slayer himself as well as his wife and daughter will be dressed. These articles, as far as the slayer is concerned, are the following: A new loin cloth (*itipi*) with a girdle of human hair (*akáchu*); a broad band, the ends of which are adorned with toucan feathers and human hair, called *itsimata*, to tie round the great pigtail at the neck; and two red-painted cotton strings with which the small braids at the temples are tied; a comb, *timashi;* ear sticks, *arusa;* pendants of brilliant beetle wings to attach to the ear lobes, called *wauo;* a crown of toucan feathers for the head, *tawasa;* an adornment for the back, made of the leg bones of the bird *tayu,* called *tayukunchi.* Of ornaments carried by the women the following are laid on the shield: A cotton string which the women tie around their hair for the feasts, *tiriangsa;* the small ear sticks of the women, *arusa;* the wooden pin which the women carry in the nether lip, *tukúnu;* a collar of beads worn around the neck, *shauka;* and some broad cotton bands tied around the upper arm, *patáki.*

Upon the shield, moreover, are placed the small pot containing juice of tobacco, a small gourd containing red ochre (*ipyáku*), three twisted cotton strings, painted red with ochre, which are to be attached to the lips of the *tsantsa,* and a knife.

After all have seated themselves the priest gives juice of tobacco to the slayer, to his wife and daughter, as well as to the medicine man, and lastly partakes of it himself. The medicine man takes the knife with the right hand and the *tsantsa* with the left and takes some juice of tobacco with the point of the knife and coats the *tsantsa* with it at the neck opening. After this he cuts off a strip of the skin from the trophy, removing nearly the whole part which formed the neck. This strip is laid down on the shield. Into the holes in the lips, where the three chonta pins had been stuck before, he inserts the three cotton strings, which are thus attached to the lips. While the medicine man is engaged in these operations the women dance round him and the other persons sit at the shield chanting their usual incantations: *chimbuyirumbá-yamáyumbá*, etc. Likewise the four warriors at the critical moments are striking their shields with the lances, performing the ceremony *yaktinyu*.

The trophy is now ready. The priest thereafter enters in action, his first task being to dress the slayer. The priest, as usual, gives him juice of tobacco through the nose and helps him to hang the *tsantsa* upon himself. Formerly it was customary among the Jibaros for the victor, before he took on the trophy, to swallow a small piece of the skin which the medicine man had cut off from the neck of the trophy, "in order to manifest that he was eating his enemy." This custom is now seldom followed, and the piece of skin is generally simply thrown away. The priest thereupon grasps the victor by the wrist, makes him take the loin cloth and the girdle, blows upon these pieces of clothing, and helps him to dress himself with them. The victor's hair is arranged. The priest helps him to comb it and to divide it into three pigtails—one large one behind and two smaller ones at the temples—which are customary among the Jibaros. The pigtails are tied around with the bands laid on the shield for this purpose. Then he in the same way receives the rest of the ornaments, the feather crown, the ear sticks, etc., from the hands of the priest, who blows upon each article before he gives it to the victor. Likewise the victor paints his face red with ochre, with the assistance of the old man.

Even the wife of the victor is ceremonially dressed by the priest, receiving from his hand the female ornaments placed on the shield.

During the whole of this dressing ceremony the women, conducted by the priestess, have been dancing and chanting around the principal persons acting.

The next thing that the victor as well as his wife and daughter have to do is to break the fast. In the women's quarters different kinds of food have previously been prepared. At a special fire *guayusa* has been cooked in a small pot. As soon as the drink is ready the priest pours a little of it into a gourd, mutters a conjuration over it and hands it to the victor, who washes his mouth with the solution, spitting it out thereafter. The priest makes the wife and daughter wash their mouths with the *guayusa* in the same way. All three are now properly purified to receive food.

Different kinds of food are brought on large banana leaves: on one leaf there is some swine's flesh, fish, and manioc, as well as a little salt and *aji*, or Indian pepper. On another banana leaf an entire boiled liver of one of the swine slaughtered has been placed. The priest gives juice of tobacco to the victor through the nose and to his wife and daughter through the mouth. Then he takes cautiously, with two fingers, a small piece of swine's flesh, mutters a conjuration over it, spits upon the ground, and gives the piece to the victor, who swallows it without touching it with his fingers. The latter subsequently receives from the hand of the old man a small piece of fish, a little manioc, as well as a pinch of salt and pepper. Thereupon the priest, with the same ceremonies, gives a little of the said dishes to the wife and daughter of the victor.

In return, the victor gives to the priest the swine's liver placed upon the other banana leaf " as a tribute of gratitude for what the priest has done for him at the feast." He handles the liver as carefully as possible, touching it merely with the tips of his fingers, and gives it to the priest, who bites off a mouthful of it. The rest of the liver is kept by the priest, who takes it to his home.

While these ceremonies have been going on the women, headed by the priestess, have been dancing and chanting around the principal persons in the way described before.

The victor having been dressed and having broken his fast, the drinking of the manioc wine, prepared with so much care, takes place. This ceremony is performed in the same way as the drinking of the manioc beer after the washing of the trophy on the previous day. The men range in two rows from the door inward, standing according to age and dignity, the oldest ones nearest to the door. The wife of the victor takes her stand in front of them in the middle of the house, holding the pot containing the wine in one hand and a small gourd in the other. The victor first steps forth to the woman and takes a draught from the gourd which she hands him. Then he goes back and fetches the priest and makes him drink in the same way from the gourd which the woman has meanwhile filled with wine. The same is repeated with each of the older warriors, who step forth by turns. After them the younger ones follow. However, according to the ceremonial only the older warriors, who themselves have killed some enemies and celebrated a victory feast, are allowed really to drink of the wine. The younger men certainly step forth to the woman, but only make a show of drinking from the gourd she holds forth and in reality do not touch it with their lips. They are not yet considered as real warriors, because they have not killed an enemy. Similarly no one of the women drinks of the liquor. What is left of the manioc wine is kept by the priest to be consumed after the meal now beginning.

After the drinking ceremony just described the general banquet takes place at which the flesh of the swine and chickens slaughtered during the night is consumed. This banquet has the same character as the meal taking place every morning after the principal ceremony of the day. However, it is considered essential that both the guests and the hosts should eat much, so that the whole supply of meat that exists is consumed. The best pieces of the swine and the chicken are selected for the victor. The meal is considered ominous for the future. Just as the victor now eats much flesh of swine and chicken, so there will not in future—thanks to the mysterious favorable influence of the *tsantsa*—be any lack of such food in his house.

After the banquet the priest distributes the remainder of the manioc wine among all the men, even the younger ones being now allowed to drink until the whole supply is exhausted.

The final ceremony still remains to be performed with the victor, in which his hair is cut and his body painted black with genipa. The priest therein acts as before. Of the great pigtail which the victor wears behind he cuts off only the last ends, but the smaller braids at the temples are completely removed. The hair cut off is laid on the shield and is kept by the victor. The hair cut on ceremonial occasions is used by the Jibaros for the preparation of the girdles of human hair which are worn by the men.

Thereupon follows the painting with genipa. A small pot containing the genipa solution is placed on the shield. The priest dips his fingers in the solution and coats the victor's whole face with it, drawing broad strokes along his breast and stomach, his back, arms, and legs. At this ceremony also the choir of the women, conducted by the priestess, assists.

Having finished these operations the priest addresses the men standing around him in much the following words: " I have completed my task as a *whuéa* at this feast. What I have done now you may also do later when you grow old."

The rest of the day is passed in the same way as during the previous days of the feast, drinking bouts being held and solo dances being performed, in which the men and the women, as usual, make their appearance by pairs. Now just as before the women generally accompany their dance with a sort of incantation.

When darkness sets in the last night's general dance commences, which is continued until dawn, when it is finished with the usual bath in the river.

Early in the morning a small drinking bout is held, whereupon the guests make themselves ready to depart and start to take leave of the hosts. The leave-taking has the same ceremonial character as the salutation at the arrival, each of the male guests addressing the victor and his relatives in a sort of speech. The words uttered, of course, have reference to the feast just finished: the splendid arrangements, the entertainment, the harmony prevailing, etc., are eulogized, and the guest in his turn invites the hosts to a visit. After this farewell ceremony, which lasts a long time, the men march off, accompanied by their wives and daughters.

After the great victory feast the Jibaro warrior generally undertakes a small journey, lasting a few days, just as he did after the previous smaller feasts. On this occasion he retires to the forest, where he stays alone, taking tobacco water, bathing every day in the waterfall, and sleeping at night in a small "dreaming hut." As soon as the black body painting has disappeared he returns home, where he finally drinks of the narcotic *maikoa* in order to see whether there are still enemies threatening him and whether everything will turn out happily for him in the future.

Concluding Remarks on the Tsantsa Feast

If we analyze the numerous ceremonies described above we find that all of them are founded upon certain fundamental ideas: (1) That in the trophy (*tsantsa*) the spirit or soul of the killed enemy is seated; (2) that the spirit, attached to the head, is thirsting for revenge and is trying to harm the slayer in every possible way; (3) that in case this danger is paralyzed through the different rites of the feast, the trophy is changed into a "fetish," a thing charged with supernatural power which the victor may make use of in different ways and in different departments of life.

The idea that the soul or vital power of a person is concentrated in his head, and particularly in his hair, seems to be common to all lower peoples in the whole world and gives the explanation not only of a number of peculiar hair customs but first of all of the practice, existing among some savage tribes, of taking the scalps of slain enemies or preparing their heads as "trophies." At any rate the use which the Jibaros make of the heads of their enemies and the ceremonies which they perform with them are throughout founded upon this idea.

Again, the idea that the spirit of a murdered man is taken by desire for revenge and that his revengeful attitude first of all is directed against the slayer is also quite natural and universally met with in the lower culture. In regard to the Jibaros, the interest is especially attached to the childish and naïve means by which the Indians fancy that they can keep the feared spirit at bay, and which are the same as those resorted to for keeping off a living human enemy. Thus the measure to keep the trophy tied to the murderous weapon, the "demoniacal" chonta lance, the rattling with the shields at the most important ceremonies, the attempts to inspire the spirit with fear by making noise, by threatening movements and dancing, and to "wash off" its malignity and desire for revenge by washing the head in a magical solution, all illustrate, in different ways, the primitive conception that the Jibaros have about the supernatural beings and the possibility of influencing them.

It seems somewhat more difficult, at first glance, to understand the fundamental idea mentioned in the third place, namely, that the trophy, in case all rites are properly performed at the feast, is turned into a real fetish and becomes a source of blessing to the slayer himself and his whole family. The power which the trophy is supposed to possess, of course, is due to the spirit attached to it, just as the natural magical power of the living human body depends upon the soul or vitality inherent in it. The souls or spirits of dead men are endowed with a special energy and potency, and among the Jibaros, as among other South American Indians, all gods, spirits, and demons seem to be nothing but departed human souls. From this point of view there is hardly anything strange in the idea that the spirit of the killed enemy, over which the victor has acquired complete domination, is able to confer upon him all those material blessings which are mentioned as the most important effects of the *tsantsa*. Among many Indian tribes in Ecuador and elsewhere there prevails the custom that the surviving relatives offer a special cult to the deceased family father, in which different kinds of food, drinks, etc., are laid upon his tomb. In case the departed spirit is satisfied with this cult, he is believed to reward his loving relatives by making their fields flourish and bear fruit, and by increasing their domestic animals; that is, by bestowing exactly the same benefits as are expected from the head trophy duly initiated. The difference between this religious act and the mode of treating the spirit of a slain enemy adopted by the Jibaro Indians appears to be that in the former case we are dealing with a real cult with offerings, while in the latter we are dealing with a purely magical conjuration which is supposed to exert an irresistible force upon the being to be influenced. That the Jibaros consider the latter means the more effective appears from the extraordinary importance ascribed to the so-called *tsantsa* feast. Some of the ceremonies at this feast also, as we have seen, have for their object to increase by artificial means the natural power of the trophy, in much the same way that an electric battery is charged with electric force.

A curious idea appears in the *tsantsa* feast, in that the victor himself on the one hand is believed to be in danger from the spirit of the killed enemy, but on the other hand, on account of his having gained possession of the enemy's head, is invested with a special mysterious power. Moreover, he is able to transfer this power by contact to other persons and to things. This explains why the victor must, in the way that we have seen, assist, for instance, at the brewing of the manioc wine for the feast and at the preparation of the sacred drink *natéma*. Similarly, something of his power is transferred to his wife and daughter and may, through them, become effective in agriculture and in other departments of life.

With a similar mysterious power the priest (*whuéa*) and the priestess (*ohāha*) are endowed. As a " priest " or conductor of the ceremonies at the feast, as stated before, only an old warrior can officiate, who himself has killed at least one enemy and celebrated a victory feast. His insight, experience, valor, and other prominent military qualities, acquired during a long life, and especially the magical power he has acquired by slaying his enemies, seems to be conceived almost as a physical reality, and his power can, like that of the victor, in a certain degree be transferred to other people. It is for this reason that he is always holding the hand of the victor at the most important ceremonies, the idea being that the action in question will thus attain more emphasis and importance. The same holds good of the priestess, through whose cooperation all actions performed by the women, and particularly by the wife and daughter of the victor, secure the tone and stress necessary.

The important rôle that the women in general play at this feast of the warriors is naturally due to the fact that the principal object of the *tsantsa* is to promote those phases of the economic life of the Indians with which the women have most to do; first of all, agriculture and the increase of the domestic animals.

The *tsantsa* of the Jibaro Indians, thus, is not a " trophy " in the common sense of the word; not exclusively a mark of distinction or a visible proof that an enemy has been killed. The Jibaro warrior not only tries to take the life of his enemy, but above everything wants to secure control of his soul. Conformably to this, the so-called *einsupani* is not merely a victory feast in the sense familiar to us, but at the same time, and first of all, a kind of mystery feast which, when we are able to penetrate into its real meaning, throws an interesting light not only upon the social life of these Indians in general and the ideas they connect with their wars, but also upon their, in some respects, rather far-reaching religious views.

2119°—23——7

INDEX